The Wonder of North American Agates

by
Dan R. Lynch & Bob Lynch

Adventure Publications
Cambridge, Minnesota

Acknowledgement

Thanks to the following for specimens and information: Allen and Amy Kraft, Eugene Mueller, Phil Burgess, Christopher Cordes, Terry Roses, Bob Anderson, and a special thank you to Jeffrey Anderson

Dedication

To Nancy Lynch and Julie Kirsch

Cover photos by Jonathan Norberg
Photographs by Dan R. Lynch

Edited by Brett Ortler
Cover design by Jonathan Norberg and Lora Westberg
Book design by Lora Westberg

10 9 8 7 6 5 4 3

The Wonder of North American Agates
Copyright © 2013 by Dan R. Lynch and Bob Lynch
Published by Adventure Publications
An imprint of AdventureKEEN
310 Garfield Street South
Cambridge, Minnesota 55008
(800) 678-7006
www.adventurepublications.net
Printed in China
ISBN 978-1-59193-415-8 (pbk.)

Table of Contents

Introduction

As colorful stones with ring-like bands, agates have been collected and admired for millennia. Enigmatic as they are beautiful, we know that they are composed of the mineral quartz but have not been able to determine exactly how they develop their characteristic banding.

Lake Superior Agate
Some of North America's most famous agates are those from the Lake Superior region

From the mountains of Brazil and the rivers of China to the frozen expanses of Siberia and the rocky peaks of Antarctica, agates are found in thousands of locations across every continent. Nevertheless, few places match the level of agate diversity found in North America, with specimens offering dramatic variations in color, patterning and mineral inclusions. Important to everyday rock hounds, serious collectors and researchers alike, the continent is an agate collecting destination and home to some of the most sought after varieties on the planet.

While North American agates represent only a fraction of the world's total agate varieties, the United States, Canada and Mexico each has much to offer. The United States boasts one of the most varied assemblages of agate types in the world, while Canada features some of the rarest agates and Mexico is home to some of the most valuable. All the while, new discoveries continue to be made in each country.

The mystery of agate formation

For as long as people have collected agates, we've wondered how they formed. Despite centuries of research and conjecture, we still don't know what causes quartz to form in such a unique way, though researchers are getting closer. Most collectors aren't concerned with the mystery, however, instead content simply to appreciate the beautiful variations found in these banded stones.

More than just stones

North American agates are more than geological curiosities; they have long been important to many cultures. Agates were worn as protective amulets during Europe's Middle Agates, ancient Egyptians used them to create ornamental beads, and over 6,000 years ago, ancient Bulgarians buried agates alongside gold in their tombs. Amazingly, their history in North America goes even further back: spearheads and knives made from agates and other forms of quartz have been found that date back over 15,000 years, older than any other human artifacts on the continent. These priceless discoveries make it clear that ours is only one of many cultures to revere agates. More importantly, these sculpted agate specimens are evidence of a remarkable chapter in human history and have shed light on the lives of the ancient peoples of the Americas.

Agates in demand

Today, agates lack much of the cultural significance they were once widely afforded, but they now represent one of the most sought after and valuable collectibles in the mineral world. Thanks to North America's many agate-producing localities, the incredible variety of specimens, and the frequent discovery of new varieties, the continent is a collector's dream.

From the most beautiful and valuable agate types to the rarest and most obscure varieties, this book is an introduction to everything North American agates have to offer. After reading it, you'll see why North America has become an agate collecting destination.

Nolte agate
A relatively new discovery of agates from Wisconsin

Understanding Agates

To appreciate agates, it helps to understand a little about them geologically. The problem is that agates are incredibly complex, and the more we learn about them, the more complex they seem to become. Another issue complicates matters: there are actually three different primary types of agates and each forms in an entirely different manner. Since we can't directly observe these types while they are forming, none are fully understood. Instead, we have to glean what we can from the existing agates themselves, including where they form, what they are made of and how they get their colors.

Oregon Coast agates
The rugged Pacific coastline of Oregon is known for its small rounded agates

What are agates?

Agates are banded mineral formations that consist primarily of chalcedony, a microscopic form of the mineral quartz. Quartz typically develops as transparent, six-sided, pointed crystals, but under certain conditions it instead grows as tiny, microscopic fiber-like crystals that are tightly packed in solid masses, resulting in a material we call chalcedony. Agates consist of highly organized layers, or bands, of both chalcedony and quartz, and it is this organization that has proved to be so difficult to explain, especially when we consider that agates form in cavities deep within rock formations.

So, what is quartz?

Quartz is a mineral, but not just any mineral: it is the most abundant mineral in the earth's crust and the most common component of many rocks, such as granite. Quartz is the crystallized (or solidified) form of silica, a common chemical compound consisting of the elements silicon and oxygen. Quartz is extremely hard and durable and is most often found in pointed crystals or rough masses, but it also frequently develops in microcrystalline varieties, such as chalcedony and agate.

Where do agates form?

Agates form within cavities in rock. These cavities range greatly in size; some agates form in vesicles (hollow gas bubbles in rock), whereas others form in long cracks and fissures. Agates also can form in several types of rock, this is one reason why so many different varieties of agates exist.

What are the varieties of agates?

Agates are popular in part because there are so many stunning agate variations. There are three primary varieties of agates, and they are derived from the types of rocks they formed within. Amygdaloidal agates (normally just called "agates") are the most common and typically formed within vesicles, cavities created by gas bubbles in cooling lava. Sedimentary agates (sometimes called "coldwater agates") grew within cavities in soft sedimentary rocks, like limestone. Finally, thunder eggs are a unique kind of agate; they have a rocky exterior and formed within cavities made by steam expanding inside pockets in volcanic rock, primarily rhyolite and tuff. The differences in these agates' appearances are as different as the rocks they formed within, yet they still all exhibit the characteristic agate banding collectors love.

What do the different names of agates mean?

No matter what your experience level, you've no doubt heard agate collectors discuss varieties of agates with interesting and sometimes strange names, like "crazy lace" and "plume agate." Within the three primary types of agates discussed above, there are many other named variations. These names derive from where an agate is found, its coloration, patterning, weathering, or its inclusions (the presence of other minerals within an agate). These variations can be thought of as "sub-varieties" of the three primary types. For example, a plume agate is one that contains plumes, which are feather- or tree-like inclusions, and they can be found in both amygdaloidal or thunder egg type agates. Similarly, "crazy lace" is the common name for a particular type of agate from a certain location in Mexico.

Brenda plume agate
Found in southwestern Arizona, Brenda plume agates are named for a nearby town

Where do agates get their colors?

By nature, quartz and chalcedony are colorless to white or gray; therefore, agates often are as well. But it is easy to see that the majority of agates are found in a wider assortment of colors. The shades of red, brown, yellow and virtually all of the other colors in an agate are caused by impurities, or tiny particles of minerals embedded within the structure of the agate. Most colors are the result of iron-bearing minerals, but compounds containing aluminum and manganese, among others, are abundant in agates as well.

Where are agates found?

Many agates are found still embedded in the rock they formed within, but depending on the area's environment and how susceptible the agates' host rock is to weathering, agates can also frequently be found loose on the ground. Agates are hard and highly resistant to weathering, so while their host rock may crumble around them, they themselves remain unchanged. As a result, they can be found in a wide array of places, everywhere from shorelines and rivers to gravel pits, mountainsides and deserts. Lake Superior agates are perhaps one of the best examples of how widespread agates can be. Originating from the Lake Superior region, glaciers pulverized the agates' host rock, freeing them and transporting them across a wide swath of land, even as far as Nebraska, hundreds of miles from where they formed. Lake Superior agates have even been found in Louisiana and the Gulf of Mexico, where they were carried by the Mississippi River.

Calandria agate
This agate originates from Chihuahua, Mexico, a major agate-producing region

How do agates form?

Trying to answer this question could fill volumes, but the truth is that despite centuries of research, we simply don't know exactly how any of the three primary types of agates formed. One issue is that chalcedony, the form of quartz that agates are composed of, is still largely misunderstood; in addition, agates form deep within rock where they cannot be

Lake Superior agate
Still embedded in basalt

observed during development. On top of that, we don't know where agates get the silica (the quartz material) that they need in order to form.

As time goes on, more theories are proposed and some of the most recent have proved to be very promising. Though the details are very complex, it seems likely that the chalcedony and quartz crystals within a developing agate organize themselves into bands as a result of chemical variations and varying speeds of crystal growth. To fully understand agate growth, however, researchers think we will need to produce a synthetic agate in a lab, where we can observe every stage of its growth. But research is slow because there is no widespread economic importance to agates and study is carried out by a dedicated few. In the meantime, we will have to be content with the present theories or, better yet, enjoy the stones for their remarkable beauty.

Mulligan Peak agate
Many of Arizona's agates are named after the hills on which they're found

A Brief Overview of
North American Agate Varieties

Fortification agates

The most abundant of all agate varieties, fortification agates are also the most popular type of agate and undoubtedly the most valuable, sought after all over North America. Fortification agates are famous for their characteristic banding, with larger bands enclosing smaller bands. Often said to resemble the walls of a castle or a fortification, these bands enclose each other as they progress inward, exhibiting the classic band-within-a-band pattern that we all think of when we imagine an agate. Not only are these the quintessential agates, fortification agates are considered to be the "truest" agates, as they formed under ideal conditions that were not present during the development of other, stranger varieties of agates. Therefore, when researchers study and postulate about agate formation, fortification agates are discussed almost exclusively. For collectors, however, a colorful, high-quality fortification agate represents the grand prize of the hobby.

Water-level agates

Often considered the antithesis of fortification agates, water-level agates certainly look different thanks to their parallel, horizontal layering. Named for their banding's resemblance to the lines made by a rising waterline, water-level agates are common but not particularly widespread throughout North America. Some localities produce countless specimens, while entire regions yield none at all. Their unique appearance is not definitively explained and many unusual theories have been put forward. The most popular theory suggests that they formed when a developing agate filled with too much water as a result of a very wet surrounding environment; instead of sticking to the sides of a cavity, the silica sank to the bottom, forming parallel bands. This aspect of water-level agates is generally agreed upon, as only gravity could have produced the characteristic horizontal bands, but most other aspects of water-level agates are a mystery. Particularly common within thunder eggs, water-level banding is very popular with collectors.

Vein agates

Though agates typically develop within cavities, not all of them do. Since they form when mineral-bearing water percolates through rock, they form wherever the conditions are right, and that can include fissures, faults and other irregular spaces, including the ragged holes groundwater makes in limestone. The often long, narrow nature of these agates lends them the name vein agates, and they can form within almost any rock type. Though not particularly abundant in North America, some vein agate varieties enjoy great popularity, while other, more obscure types are interesting curiosities. They are an example of an agate variety that is best appreciated when found still embedded in their host rock, because once they are weathered free they look like any other agate. Perhaps this is the reason why they are not widely popular, though their elongated, often jagged patterns give us a beautifully unique insight into how different types of agates form.

Eye agates

Collectors spend a lot of time staring at agates, but only one variety seems to stare back. Eye agates, sometimes called fish-eye or bull's-eye agates are appropriately termed, as they exhibit perfectly round, circular banded features. Every once in a while, a specimen may even have features that look uncannily similar to eyes, complete with an "iris" and a "pupil." It is for this reason that eye agates are among the most popular and endearing varieties of agates. But agate eyes are also unique features for other reasons; they typically only form on the outer surfaces of an agate, and despite how round the eyes may be, they are not actually spheres, but hemispheres, or half-spheres.

This means that if an agate is heavily weathered or polished too aggressively, the eyes are worn away. But for all their value and desirability, eyes are not very rare on agates; whether they are coin-sized or nearly microscopic, eyes can be found on many agates from around North America.

Agate geodes

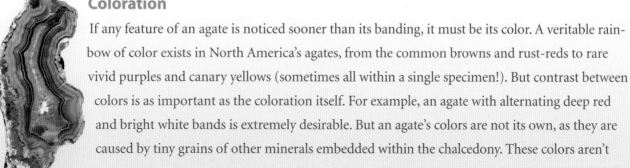

A geode is any rounded, hollow geological formation. Despite this seemingly simple definition, they can be composed of almost any material, making for countless varieties of geodes. Most geodes consist of various kinds of rock while others consist entirely of a single mineral. Thanks to the different ways agates can form, agate geodes can fall into either category. Some agate geodes are just that—hollow agates. While rare, the hollow interior of these "unfinished" agates can even contain growths of other minerals, such as calcite. Thunder eggs, on the other hand, are rocky masses of rock that contain a lining of agate around their hollow cores. Not all thunder eggs are hollow, but geodes are quite common at thunder egg agate localities. Despite the key differences between thunder eggs and "unfinished agates," both are considered agate geodes and are enjoyed by collectors, especially those who cut specimens open to discover the surprises that may hide within.

Coloration

If any feature of an agate is noticed sooner than its banding, it must be its color. A veritable rainbow of color exists in North America's agates, from the common browns and rust-reds to rare vivid purples and canary yellows (sometimes all within a single specimen!). But contrast between colors is as important as the coloration itself. For example, an agate with alternating deep red and bright white bands is extremely desirable. But an agate's colors are not its own, as they are caused by tiny grains of other minerals embedded within the chalcedony. These colors aren't necessarily constant, either. As the mineral grains are weathered by acidic water, faded by the sunlight, oxidized upon exposure to air or stained by other minerals, the color of an agate can change and evolve, sometimes drastically. When a locality produces agates known especially for unusual coloration, the location becomes known for it, sometimes above all else. This can occur when agates vary radically in color from specimen to specimen, show uniquely vivid hues or exhibit pronounced color changes resulting from weathering.

Moss agates

Before the late 1700s, when agates were not yet being widely studied, people looked at the wild, twisting growths within moss agates and concluded they looked so organic that it had to be fossilized moss trapped within the chalcedony. Today, we know that the "moss" in moss agates is actually a series of tiny mineral-filled tubes created by elaborate and beautiful chemical reactions. But to most collectors, moss agates are simply some of the most stunning examples of inclusions in agates, but they are also the most common, as most agate-producing localities yield moss formations. The most desirable specimens contain little sections of banded agate tucked between the mossy growths. And while they may not be the most valuable of agate varieties, they remain one of the most popular types. Widely used in jewelry, moss agates still provoke the imagination. Even today, when we know how the "moss" was actually formed, it's easy to entertain the 300-year-old idea that something organic may lie within.

Plume agates

To a certain segment of agate collectors, not even the most perfect fortification or water-level agate can compare to the beauty of a world-class plume agate. While that may seem strange to some, these fanatics may have the right idea; plume agates offer a sense of imagery and depth that few other agates can evoke. Plumes, named for their similarity to plumes of smoke or feathers, are growths caused by mineral particles free-floating in a solution, building upon each other when they contact one another. While it is not completely understood how they form within agates, their elaborate three-dimensional structure tells us that they developed when the agate was in a non-solid state. This is no better illustrated than when a specimen is polished, letting us see that well-formed plumes seem to float within the agate, gracefully suspended, often diving deeper and out of sight. When combined with their rarity, this artful appearance makes plume agates a popular variety of agate.

Sagenitic agates

Despite the insistence of some collectors, there is actually no mineral called "sagenite" (pronounced SAJ-en-ite). When that name was originally devised in 1796, it referred to the titanium-bearing mineral we know today as rutile, which forms crystals shaped like long, slender needles. Over time, the definition changed and "sagenite" became the term for any needle-like crystals embedded within quartz, no matter what mineral they were actually composed of. Today, as the word continues to evolve, we now say that agates are "sagenitic" when they contain sagenite formations and exhibit the spearlike shapes of other minerals, such as goethite, anhydrite and zeolites. Sometimes these crystals are displayed in beautiful and colorful circular or fan-shaped arrangements, making it clear why agates with inclusions are often popular. Though sagenitic agates are more common in some parts of North America and they range in desirability and value, they are always appreciated among serious collectors.

Inclusions

Agates rarely form alone. While the conditions for agate formation are believed to be very specific, dozens of other minerals that aren't nearly as finicky are able to grow within cavities both before and during an agate's development. As they compete for the limited space, these other minerals, such as calcite and goethite, can eventually become embedded within the final agate as a mineral inclusion—sagenitic agates (see page 15) are a specific example of this. But this is not a simple process, and the other minerals aren't overtaken so easily. The developing agates warp and bend around the crystals and growths already present. Some mineral inclusions later succumb to weathering and dissolve, leaving geometric cavities in their place, while others are impregnated by silica (quartz material) over time, turning them to quartz. However they appear, a certain portion of collectors pride themselves on collecting the strangest, most interesting and rarest mineral inclusions in agates.

Fossil Replacements

Agates require a cavity in which to form, but as long as the basic conditions for their formation are met, the type of cavity is largely irrelevant. Vein agates (see page 12), which form within cracks in rock, are a good example of this. Perhaps the most interesting place an agate can form, one which often surprises newcomers to agate collecting, is within fossils. Some develop much like any other agate—within a void in rock—except in this case the void was formerly occupied by decayed organic material, such as wood. Others result from chalcedony slowly replacing the cells of rigid structures, like coral. Called replacements or agatized fossils, these agates may form in several ways, but the outcome is the same: agates with the shape of ancient plants or animals. They are rare in North America (and everywhere else, for that matter), which makes them very sought after and valuable, both as agate specimens and as artifacts from the ancient world.

Weathered agates

Consider the life of an agate: it formed in darkness within solid rock hundreds of millions of years ago and spent eons entombed within the shifting earth, until its host rock was finally exposed by the weather and thrust into the elements, where the host rock was slowly worn down into dust. Along the way, earthquakes, volcanic heat, acids, freeze and thaw cycles, moving water, ice and wind all took their toll on agates. Finding an agate before it disappears forever is a fortunate event—as much for the agate as for the finder—but many specimens bear the scars of the history they have endured. Many distinct weathering effects are even considered separate agate varieties. Water-washed agates are one example; these agates have been completely rounded after millennia of rolling around in rivers. Faulted agates are another type of "weathered agate." They were broken but then "healed" by quartz, often leaving their bands misaligned. However they weathered, agates can't hide their pasts, and we, as collectors, should take notice of all that they've gone through.

Map of North American Agates

Agates are distributed far and wide across North America and are found at hundreds of localities. From beaches to outcroppings of solid rock, each locality yields agates with traits and characteristics as unique as the geologic environment that produced them. This is why each locality is said by collectors to produce a different variety of agate. But an agate's locality is more than just the place it came from; it becomes an agate's identity. An agate is bought, sold and collected based largely on the knowledge of where it came from and therefore what variety it is. To lose this information is to render an agate "homeless," not only depriving it of its varietal name but robbing it of its collectibility and value, effectively turning it from a unique and desirable agate into merely a colorful stone.

This map shows just a small fraction of North America's agates and where they are found. While more agates certainly come from the western portions of the continent than the east, no region is devoid of them. Even in areas in which few or no agates are known, such as some of Canada's northern reaches, the lack of agates is most often attributed to the remoteness of the area or because collecting is not allowed because the land is protected. In other words, it's likely that agates are there, too. Generally speaking, in North America, you're never too far from an agate locality, whether the agates formed there or were carried there by weathering. In either case, you can be sure it has its own distinct name.

Note: The map to the right indicates general areas where the agates are found and not necessarily a specific locality. While some of these agates are found in very restricted locations, others can be found across much of a region. This map represents only a fraction of the continent's agates.

Agates of the Western United States

Dryhead agate
The intense coloration dryhead agates makes them one of Montana's best-known varieties

Agates
of the Western United States

The western half of the United States is, without a doubt, North America's premier region for agate collecting. Hundreds, if not thousands, of varieties are known from these western states and more are discovered each year. From obscure mountainside outcroppings to legendary desert mines, the region produces more agates and agate varieties than most other regions of North America combined. Here we will discuss the most famous agates the West has to offer, such as Baker Ranch thunder eggs and Dryhead agates, along with some of the rarest.

Baker Ranch thunder eggs

Thunder eggs have rough, rocky exteriors, and many localities don't produce specimens with well-developed patterns or attractive colors. This may be why some serious agate collectors think of thunder eggs as a curiosity or a niche collectible unworthy of their primary collection. But Baker Ranch thunder eggs are colorful and valuable enough to convince almost any skeptic. These thunder eggs shatter all preconceptions about this compelling subset of agates. Found in the Baker Ranch area in southern New Mexico, these agates come from land that is privately claimed, making the dark green, red and black agates rare and very valuable. Many finds turn out to be hollow geodes when cut open, but specimens with solid fortification-banded interiors are second to none when it comes to North American thunder eggs.

Baker Ranch thunder egg
These dark fortification agates are
New Mexico's most desirable specimens.

Baker Ranch thunder egg
Some Baker Ranch geodes contain stalactites of quartz

Valuable Finds Not only is Baker Ranch possibly the best-known thunder egg agate locality in North America, it also produces some of the most valuable specimens. The locality actually consists of several thunder egg-producing rock beds in southern New Mexico, and their significance and value have not gone unnoticed; this is evidenced by the fact that the entire area is privately claimed. There is a tremendous variety among specimens, and though the best are entirely banded, a large number of Baker Ranch agates are geodes. Interesting formations of quartz are often found within these Baker Ranch geodes. The quartz is not simply a lining, but occurs as intergrown towers or stalactites (icicle-like formations) of tiny crystals. Combined with the characteristic coloration of Baker Ranch agates, these geodes are among the finest thunder egg specimens in the Southwest.

Big Diggings agate
Black and red "moody" coloration is
the trademark of Big Diggings agates

Big Diggings agates

The curiously named Big Diggings locality is a series of agate collecting sites that
produce everything from fortification agates to moss and plume agates. But the
agates that have kept collectors coming back for most of the twentieth century are
those with the locality's trademark dark colorations, featuring stunning bluish
gray, black and blood-red hues. These splotchy, inky tints evoke a moodiness not
found in many other North American agates, making the agates from this New
Mexico location desirable even decades after they were first discovered. Most are
rimmed with a white layer of softer minerals, particularly calcite, and some
specimens contain a central core of clear quartz crystals. But it is the vivid yet
uneven red coloration, caused by iron-rich groundwater staining the chalcedony,
that makes Big Diggings agates some of the most attractive in the Southwest.

Odd agates with an odder name Dozens of different varieties of agates are found in New Mexico, including some amazing plume agates. The Big Diggings area is renowned for producing some of the finest plume agates in the state, as well as some of the most mineralogically interesting specimens. Unlike most other plume agates, Big Diggings agates often have thin, twig-like plumes and rounded, feathery plumes together in the same specimen; this likely signifies two distinct periods of plume development. Other plume agates found elsewhere in North America generally consist of plumes floating in unbanded chalcedony, but Big Diggings plume agates are often more varied, containing banding and quartz crystals as well. Big Diggings plume agates aren't common, though, so unless you plan on going to collect them yourself, you may have trouble finding good specimens for sale.

Big Diggings plume agate
Two distinct kinds of plumes are visible in this interesting specimen

Black agate thunder egg
An example of how shifting of the earth can cause non-parallel layering

Black agate thunder eggs

Many agate varieties are found in the Wiley's Well geological district near Blythe, California, but black agate thunder eggs are among the most interesting. As their name suggests, black agate thunder eggs are well known for their dark coloration, but they are especially fascinating because their water-level bands often exhibit layers that are not parallel with one another. The horizontal banding seen in typical water-level agates formed when gravity pulled agate-producing silica down to the bottom of a cavity, where it settled in parallel bands. The tilted bands seen in black agate thunder eggs therefore could only occur if the agate was tilted while it was still forming. Earthquakes and other tectonic movement are the most likely cause for this unique feature of black agate thunder eggs, which makes them one of the highly sought after curiosities of North America's agates.

Brownsville agates

If you're a collector of sagenitic agates, Brownsville, Oregon, is a locality that you should know about. Located in the vicinity of several other prolific agate localities, Brownsville produces some of the best sagenitic agates in North America, with specimens exhibiting well-preserved needles encased within or, in the case of some spectacular examples, actually extending out beyond the boundaries of the agate. Those familiar with the minerals of Oregon will know that the state is distinctly known for its specimens of zeolites, which are minerals that formed in volcanic rocks as they were altered by groundwater. Many of Oregon's zeolites form as delicate needle-like crystals, and it is growths like these that are thought to be embedded in Brownsville's agates. While Brownsville's sagenites are not known to be particularly colorful, these agates are still coveted by sagenite collectors.

Brownsville sagenitic agate
Common near Brownsville, many sagenitic agates appear to contain zeolite minerals

Dryhead agates

Dryhead agates are an "old time" variety, beloved for decades as one of the most desirable agate types in North America. They are found in the vicinity of the Bighorn River in southern Montana, just a few miles north of the Wyoming border, where they are mined from the arid hills of the Pryor Mountains. Their interesting name stems from a wealth of dried buffalo skulls said to have been present below the cliffs where the agates were first found; others say they were named for Dryhead Canyon, in Wyoming, just south of the locality. They are sedimentary agates, formed within limestone and shale as hard, rocky ball-like formations called concretions that show no banding until cut open.

Dryhead agates are famous for their well-formed fortification patterns, but they are even better known for their coloration. Virtually every specimen is colored in distinct shades of reddish orange, white and, rarely, lavender, making Dryheads one of the very few agate varieties that can be reliably identified by color alone. Today, Dryheads are only found on private land, which drives up the value of specimens already on the market.

Dryhead agate
Characteristic in color and shape, dryhead agates are easily recognizable

Dryhead agate
Most dryheads have complete, well-formed fortification patterns

Dugway geode
Intricate banding surrounds a quartz-lined geode cavity; specimens like this are common

Dugway geodes

If one were to list North America's finest varieties of thunder egg agates, Utah's Dugway geodes would certainly make the top ten. Found in the Dugway Mountains for which they are named, a large percentage are hollow, hence their common label "Dugway geodes" rather than the more accurate "Dugway thunder eggs." Most are banded in soft shades of gray, white or blue, and the rocky shell surrounding a specimen is often as beautifully patterned as the agate itself. For decades they've been dug out of weathered rock and clay, and though some specimens consist entirely of banded chalcedony, hollow specimens have historically been most popular. When it comes to agate collecting, this is unique; in most other agate localities, hollow specimens are usually less desirable than solid agates. Perhaps it's because these geodes are almost always lined with countless tiny quartz crystals that sparkle like sugar, making Dugway geodes beloved by collectors of all skill levels.

Fairburn agate
Polishing a Fairburn agate, even when it is rough and broken, is always frowned upon by serious collectors

Fairburn agates

Only a few other varieties of North American agates are as renowned as Fairburn agates. Named for the little town of Fairburn, South Dakota, Fairburn agates are found primarily in the hills and valleys of the harsh, hot Black Hills region, where the rugged terrain hides these extremely rare gems. They can be so difficult to find, in fact, that diehard collectors sometimes camp in the area for days to collect just a single specimen. But it isn't just their rarity that makes Fairburns famous, they can also be stunningly beautiful. With vivid, contrasting colors and sharply delineated patterns, they are some of North America's most attractive examples of fortification agates. But their fame and rarity is not without its drawbacks for amateurs; the price of a high-quality specimen—even one as small as a thumbnail—is sure to make your jaw drop, as Fairburns are among the most valuable varieties on the continent.

Needles in a haystack Fairburn agates formed within limestone and are therefore sedimentary in nature. Recent studies suggest that they developed within cavities that originally were occupied by masses of calcite, which weathered away. But when Fairburns are collected, they are nearly always free of their host rock, found buried in gravel and sand instead, where they are more easily weathered. In fact, the exteriors of Fairburn agates often appear smoothed and shiny due to millennia of blowing sand. The best specimens consist entirely of agate

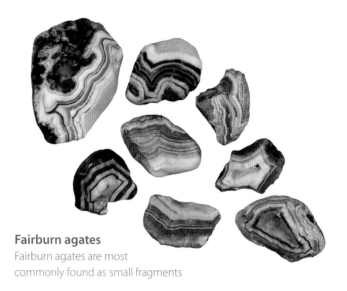

Fairburn agates
Fairburn agates are most commonly found as small fragments

Fairburn agate
A large amount of specimens consist of small portions of banding within chert or other quartz materials

banding, but many exhibit only small banded areas within a larger mass of non-agate quartz material. Still, wherever there is banding, it is typically described as having "holly leaf" patterning, due to its resemblance to the curving shapes and sharp points of a holly leaf. No matter the quality of a specimen, finding an elusive Fairburn agate is often seen as a sort of "badge of honor" among Midwestern rock hounds and the mark of an accomplished, committed (or just plain lucky) collector.

Filigree agates

Exemplifying all of the key characteristics of moss agates, filigree agates live up to their name thanks to their elaborate strands and knots of thread-like growths. Found in central Idaho, filigree agates are mined on a private claim, but the mine owners produce beautiful specimens and bring them to the market. Filigree agates formed as veins within rhyolite, and most are light-colored with gray or colorless chalcedony that is filled with attractive mint-green mossy growths. This coloration is interesting because it is replicable in a simple lab experiment; placing grains of a compound called ferrous sulfate into a body of silica-rich gel starts a chemical reaction that produces moss-like growths of a similar green color. A similar process seems to have led to the formation of moss agates, and finding moss agates with a similar coloration supports the theory.

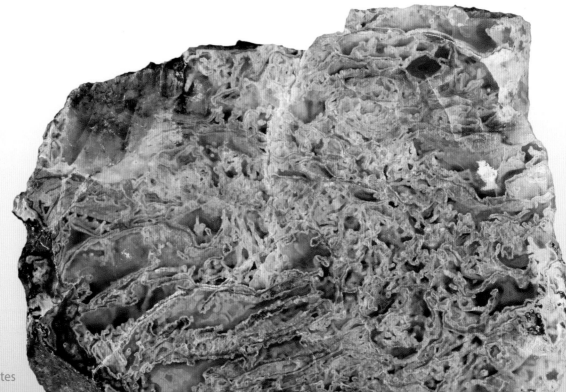

Filigree agate
The moss in Filigree agate
is typically a rich green

Fourth of July Butte agates

Arizona is home to many different varieties of agates—many more than most states—so it seems a little ironic that one of the best-known types from the state contains very little color. Fourth of July Butte, west of Phoenix, is littered with agate nodules that, when cut or polished, reveal perfectly formed fortification patterns with surprisingly little color. Most are white or gray, but a rare few are light blue or have rich brown outer layers. With such well-defined banding and nice patterns, their lack of any significant coloration isn't a detriment to their collectibility. Even better for collectors, they are fairly affordable and easy to acquire. Like any good agate locality, however, private claims mean many of the best collecting grounds are off-limits.

Fourth of July Butte agates
These specimens are typical examples of Fourth of July Butte agates

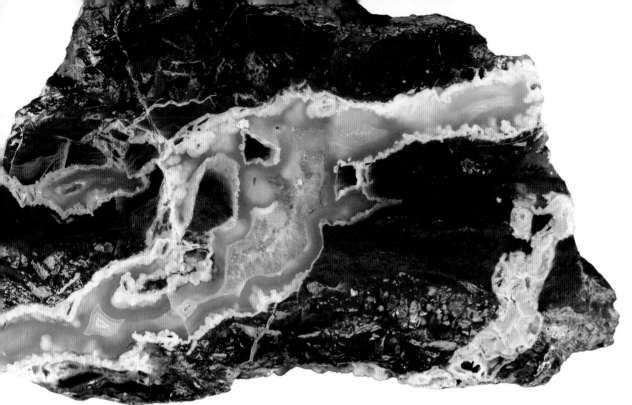

Grant Creek agate
The translucent gray section of this specimen is actually a newer agate, formed among the rubble of a brown, older agate

Grant Creek agates

The agates from the Grant Creek area in Idaho are a great example of the agates produced at privately owned mining claims. At these sites, passionate collectors meticulously extract specimens, bringing otherwise rare, remote and isolated agate varieties to the market where the average collector can obtain a specimen. Grant Creek agates are found as banded veins that fill fissures in colorful, highly altered rhyolite. Like any vein agate, they filled the ragged spaces available to them, often cross-cutting the layers of their host rock, which makes for striking specimens. But some Grant Creek agates have an even more interesting feature: the addition of a distinct second generation of agate growth.

Idaho's vein agates When an agate is crushed, it is not always destroyed. If an earthquake, high pressure or another force breaks up an agate while it is still deeply embedded in its host rock, silica solutions can later flow into it and crystallize, effectively repairing the agate. But, rarely, those secondary solutions form an agate of their own, resulting in something truly unique: two visually distinct generations of agate growth within the same specimen. Some of the vein agates from the Grant Creek area in Idaho exhibit this amazing characteristic and make extremely interesting specimens for study when cut and polished. In these examples, misaligned sections of shattered agate banding surround intact agate patterns. To an untrained eye, these specimens can appear merely as odd, jumbled agates, but to observant collectors, these rarities can be a remarkable addition to your shelf.

Grant Creek agate
Some vein agates from Grant Creek exhibit inclusions, such as plumes

Graveyard Point plume agates

In recent years, plume agates from the Graveyard Point area of Oregon have gained significant popularity thanks to a very active mining operation that is bringing specimens to the market. Using heavy equipment, specimens are excavated from veins and cavities still buried underground. Under a mile from the Idaho border, this agate-producing site is remote. As if the difficulty of mining the specimens and accessing the site were not enough, the site is privately owned and closed to the average agate collector. Graveyard Point plume agates appear in a variety of colors and typically lack any banding, but like other kinds of plume agates, slicing them reveals the large, beautiful feather-like growths within them. They can be quite large, with some measuring several feet in size. So while we must rely on professional rock hounds to sell Graveyard Point agates to us, the results are worth the price.

Graveyard Point plume agate
Large, sweeping plumes and a unique opaque coloration make this a fine example of a Graveyard Point agate

Hauser Bed thunder egg
Partial water-level patterns are
common in these agates

Hauser Bed thunder egg agates

West of the city of Blythe, in one of the hottest
regions of southern California, lies Wiley's Well,
an area with natural hot springs that produce
mineral-bearing water heated to over 90 degrees.
The area is rich with thunder egg agates, and
today's springs are but a remnant of the ancient
volcanic activity that produced them. Different
sites in the vicinity of the well each yield their
own variety of thunder egg, but the best-known
localities are the Hauser beds, which have been
worked for agates since the 1930s. Typically
grayish blue in color, the banding within their
rocky shells is often of the water-level type,
occasionally with a hollow geode cavity above
the banding. Specimens still turn up from this
historic locality, and fine specimens still excite
collectors, even after all this time.

Holly blue agates

Oregon is host to a seemingly endless variety of agates, with specimens in all colors of the rainbow, but holly blue agates are one of the few types in the state colored in shades of purple. Found in the hills near the town of Sweet Home in western Oregon, these unique little agates are dug out of veins and cavities in rhyolite and exhibit delicate, faint banding. Though they're best known for their subtle lavender hues, less desirable specimens are true to their name and are found in shades of grayish blue.

Holly blue agate
This small polished specimen
shows the usual color

Little Florida Mountains thunder egg agates

The Little Florida Mountains, just southeast of Deming, New Mexico, are a treasure trove of thunder egg agates. There is even Rock Hound State Park on the western side of the mountains, founded specifically as a place for agate collectors to hunt for thunder eggs. There are a number of other dig sites in the Little Florida Mountains as well, many of which are private claims. Each site produces distinct thunder eggs, but thanks to their shared origin, there are similarities between them, too. For example, the rocky shells that surround the agates are typically reddish brown with lighter-colored stripes and layers, and the chalcedony banding is most often gray, white or bluish. A great many are also geodes with central cavities lined with quartz crystals. With evocative names like "sugar bowl thunder eggs," "blue sky thunder eggs" and "wormhole thunder eggs," the Little Florida Mountains are a source of an exciting array of agates and a popular source of agate geodes.

Little Florida Mountains thunder egg
This is an example of a "wormhole thunder egg," one of the many varieties found in the area

Marfa agates

Marfa, Texas, may be more famous for the "Marfa lights" UFO phenomenon, but the surrounding area also produces more believable wonders: agates. Specimens from Marfa vary in terms of appearance and structure, but those containing inclusions tend to garner the most attention. Many contain plumes, dendrites or moss, sometimes all in the same specimen, and these features contrast with beautifully colored chalcedony.

Marfa agate
This unusually bluish specimen contains black moss and plume formations

Marfa agate
Sharp-tipped plume formations on the edge of a Marfa agate's banded pattern

Plume agates from Marfa, Texas, are rare and are consequently not as widely known or as popular as they should be. Specimens often contain bright, highly visible plumes with uniquely pointed tips, and collectors with a microscope could spend a whole day poring over the details of a single agate. If nothing else, Marfa plume agates are proof that even the lesser-known and more obscure agates are still worthy of attention.

Montana moss agate
The daub-like, intermittent brown coloration of this specimen is common

Montana moss agates

As one of North America's legendary agate varieties, Montana moss agates have been collected and cherished for most of the past century. In fact, Montana moss agates are so ubiquitous in agate collections that it is impossible to discuss the continent's agates without mentioning them. But their name, as historic as it may be, is a bit of a misnomer, as the majority do not contain traditional agate "moss." They do, however, exhibit other, perhaps more exciting, inclusions, particularly dendrites. Dendrites are mineral formations that develop within the microscopic cracks and spaces in agates and form as branching tree-like growths. Appropriately enough, dendrites get their name from the Greek word *déndron*, which translates to "tree." In Montana moss agates, dendrites are abundant and take two forms: delicate fern-like growths and large irregular or rounded flattened masses, both of which give these agates the general appearance of being overgrown with spots of moss, lending them their famous name.

Montana moss agate
The black shapes in this specimen
are actually irregular dendrites

Gray agates from the Yellowstone River Montana moss agates are found primarily along the Yellowstone River in eastern Montana, where they are collected as smooth-surfaced stones, some up to a foot or more in size. On the outside, Montana moss agates are rather uninteresting and gray to brown in color, but when cut open, they are spectacular, with black dendrites, plumes and moss amid pale, faint banding and brown or honey-colored wisps and smears of color. For decades, Montana moss agate collectors have sliced their finds like loaves of bread because every slice reveals different dendritic patterns. Each section is different because of the nature of dendrites, which formed when mineral-bearing water seeped into the tiny voids, fractures and microscopic spaces between layers of chalcedony. Practically speaking, this makes dendrites essentially two-dimensional. Sliced or not, Montana moss agate's translucent chalcedony often allows us to see deeper into agates, enabling us to see the beautiful dendrites and other inclusions hiding below.

Unique Coloration While dendrites are the Montana moss agate's main attraction, their coloration is also interesting. Though most are gray with little variation other than their characteristic black spots, some show beautiful "smears" of honey-brown or black across their bands. These specimens are noteworthy, as the coloration is typically found isolated on just a segment of the banding, not across entire bands. Nearby bands often look alike and are unevenly colored in the same portion of the agate. This suggests that these color-causing impurities were introduced later, probably as a result of iron-rich groundwater seeping into cracks in the agate and staining sections of the banding.

Montana moss agate
This beautiful pair of dendrites
exhibits striking symmetry

Nebraska blue agates

Nebraska isn't a state that is widely known for agates. Occasional finds of Lake Superior agates transported to the state by glaciers or Fairburn agates from South Dakota found in gravel or along riverbeds are generally the extent of Nebraska agate collecting. But not all of Nebraska's agates came from elsewhere, and at least one variety, the Nebraska blue agate, is native to the state. Found in Sioux County in the same formation of sedimentary rock that makes up much of South Dakota's Badlands region, this rare, lesser-known variety of agate is found in dark shades of gray and black that can appear bluish in sunlight, giving them their name. They exhibit faint fortification patterns and rough, irregular exteriors. But despite their rarity, these agates are not especially valuable, thanks to their dark coloration.

Nebraska blue agate
Most specimens only exhibit their name-sake blue coloration in bright sunlight

Needle Peak agates

Western Texas is known for producing all kinds of agates, particularly those with interesting inclusions such as sagenites, plumes and, of course, moss. The area around Needle Peak in Brewster County is prime hunting ground for spectacular moss agates, which turn up as grayish masses of banded chalcedony littered with bright green mossy growths, often only around the edges of the agate. These agates are a delight to view under magnification, as all the twists and turns of the elaborate, delicate moss growths are visible in great detail as they tunnel deeper into the agate. But as interesting and beautiful as they are, Needle Peak's moss agates are not the primary focus of area agate collectors—that honor goes to the area's peculiar "pompom" agates, which contain yellow "fuzz balls" of sagenite formations.

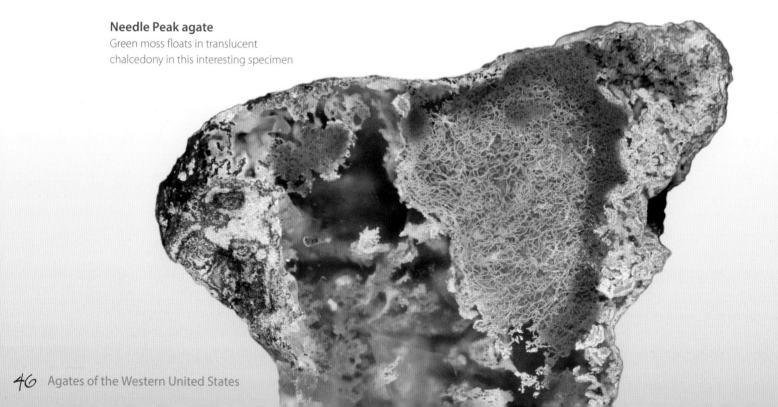

Needle Peak agate
Green moss floats in translucent chalcedony in this interesting specimen

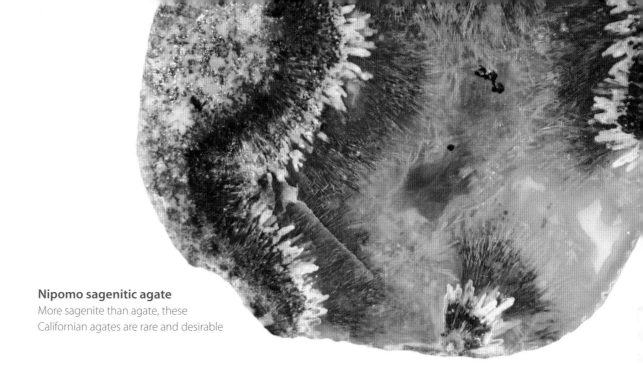

Nipomo sagenitic agate
More sagenite than agate, these
Californian agates are rare and desirable

Nipomo sagenitic agates

Once abundant in dealers' stock but now difficult to come by, Nipomo sagenitic agates are a famous and popular "old time" variety of agate. Named for the town of Nipomo, California, located northeast of Los Angeles, these agates are also called "bean field agates" because they would be found in bean fields when farmers turned the soil each year. They were once found in the vicinity of Nipomo, all the way west to the Pacific coast, but the land is no longer farmed or worked as it once was, and the supply of specimens has all but dried up as a result. But rather than fade into obscurity like many other "lost" varieties of agates, they are still sought after thanks to their beautifully detailed and well-formed bundles of embedded crystals. Indeed, these stunning sagenitic agates have solidified their place in North America's agate collecting history.

Nipomo sagenitic agate
These are some of the finest sagenitic agates on the continent

Textbook examples Nipomo's sagenitic agates are considered some of the best sagenitic agates for a few reasons. First, the needle-shaped crystals are textbook examples of sagenite formations: they are long, slender and arranged into divergent "spray-shaped" groups. On top of that, the grayish chalcedony in between the sagenitic growths is typically so translucent that the crystals can be seen even when deep within the agate, offering a sense of depth that gives specimens an almost sculptural or organic quality. Nipomo sagenitic agates are generally cut in half and polished flat so that these traits can be best appreciated. And though these agates hardly exhibit any variation in color and samples are often fairly small, even average specimens can fetch high prices, thanks in part to their historic collectibility.

Oregon eye agates

Western Oregon is home to many varieties of agates, some of which are much better known than others. Oregon eye agates are one of the more obscure examples and exhibit small green and gray eyes of chalcedony on the surfaces of small white agates. Collectors tend to polish them on all sides to reveal all of the eyes each specimen has to offer. Even though these agates are uncommon, they typically aren't valuable, though this doesn't make them any less desirable to many eye agate collectors.

Oregon eye agate
A typical specimen of these uncommon and interesting eye agates

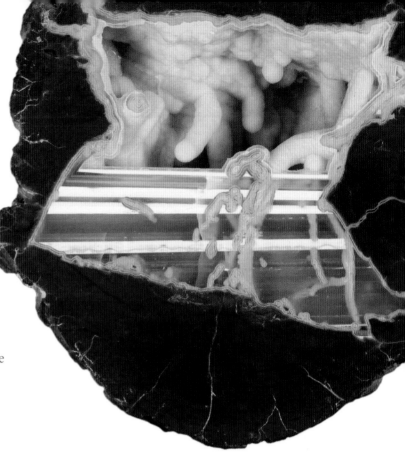

Richardson Ranch thunder egg
Extremely rare chalcedony "worms" are one of the possible prizes in these geodes

Oregon thunder egg agates

Oregon is known worldwide for its thunder eggs, and many localities in the state produce distinct varieties. Richardson Ranch, Priday Ranch and Friend Ranch are just a few of the thunder egg destinations you'll hear of again and again. No matter the locality, however, not all of the thunder eggs are solid. Many are hollow geodes, the most interesting of which are "unfinished" water-level agates with a flat agate "floor" or those that contain chalcedony-coated inclusions that look like tubes or "worms" dangling in the chamber. Oregon thunder eggs are regarded as some of the best agate geodes in North America, and colorful specimens can be of considerable value. As with any thunder egg, cutting an Oregon egg is like opening a treasure chest; the beautiful banding and delicate features hidden within the rough, lumpy, ugly exterior never cease to surprise and amaze even long-time collectors.

Oregon: the thunder egg capital of North America Thunder egg agates are found all over central Oregon, and whether they are filled with fortification banding, water-level banding, moss or plumes, you can never know what will be inside a specimen until you cut it open. Tubes are one type of inclusion that can be found in the state's thunder eggs, especially those near Madras, Oregon. Though they are typically considered undesirable by local collectors, fans of agates with unique inclusions love them for their interesting, detailed growths. In most specimens, the tubes probably formed much like the "moss" in moss agates: the result of a chemical reaction that was then later coated in chalcedony. Cutting or polishing these stones allows us to see these structures in cross-section, revealing their tube-like nature. Because of their "weird" nature, tube agates are not worth much, but clever rock hounds can use this to their advantage and quickly build an affordable collection of fantastic tube agates.

Madras thunder egg
Often found in a collector's "junk" bin, thunder eggs with dense tube formations are unusual and very interesting

Priday plume agate
This close-up shows the intricacies of some of North America's finest plume agates

Oregon plume agates

The plume agates found in central Oregon are some of the most celebrated on the planet. Two of the prime localities are Priday Ranch, near Madras, and Robinson Ranch, near Prineville. Both are privately owned areas that have produced incredible plume agates prized by collectors. Priday Ranch is particularly noteworthy, as it is the source of "Priday plume" thunder egg agates. Today, Priday Ranch is part of the famous Richardson Ranch, which encompasses several thunder egg-producing outcrops and rock beds that were once distinctly named localities. While many of the old site names have faded from popular usage in favor of the Richardson Ranch name, the "Priday plume agate" name persists thanks to their famously well-formed and beautiful smoke-like plumes. Some of the finest and rarest Priday specimens contain brightly colored plumes in shades of yellow and red, though most are dark colored.

Unbelievable—and valuable—plume agates Like the Priday Ranch area, Robinson Ranch is a large agate-producing area off-limits to the average collector, but it still supplies the agate collecting community with amazingly detailed plume agates. Both Priday plumes and Robinson Ranch plume agates are "old time" varieties from North America, prized by collectors since the mid-1900s. Though whole specimens tend to be more valued today, it was once commonplace for collectors to cut specimens extensively in order to reveal the best plumes hiding within an agate. This resulted in agates that were sawn repeatedly, as if dissected. Such pieces were then frequently used in jewelry, backlit in a collector's display case, or simply stowed away like treasure. Today, these localities are less actively collected, but the pillowy and often colorful Priday plumes and dark, branching Robinson Ranch plumes can still be found at rock shows, especially those in the western United States, where they fetch high prices.

Robinson Ranch plume agate
A close-up of the minute details found in Oregon's plume agates

Paulina limb casts

Oregon has a long history of volcanic activity, and this violent geological past is evidenced by its rocky peaks and sheets of lava that cover thousands of square miles. Millions of years ago, a volcanic eruption took place in a forested area around Paulina in central Oregon. While that in itself isn't unusual, when the molten rock and hot ash contacted the trees, the moisture in the wood hardened the rock, creating limb-shaped shells. As the wood inside burned or rotted away, hollow rock casts of the tree limbs remained, which would later serve as the cavities in which agates could form. Typically faintly banded, grayish pink in color, and often containing many mineral inclusions, Paulina limb casts retain the outward appearance of wood and tree bark so well that they are often confused for fossilized wood, when in reality they are much rarer and more valuable.

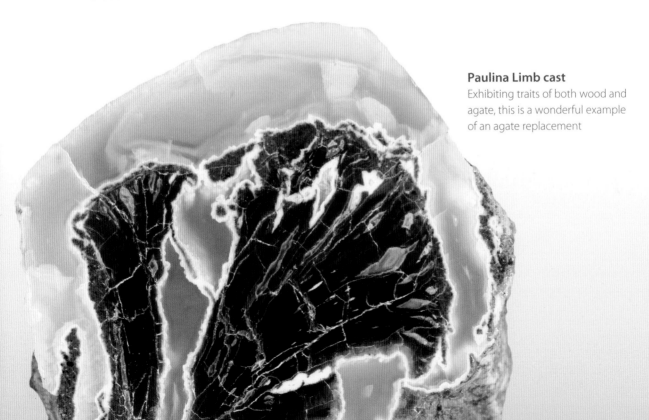

Paulina Limb cast
Exhibiting traits of both wood and agate, this is a wonderful example of an agate replacement

Richardson Ranch thunder egg
Translucent layers give a sense of depth, allowing a view to the structures hidden below

Richardson Ranch thunder egg
Water-level patterns are common and abundant but interesting and beautiful

Richardson Ranch thunder eggs
Moss-filled specimens exemplify the type yet still aren't desired by local collectors

Richardson Ranch thunder egg agates

The dramatic volcanic activity that shaped Oregon produced huge amounts of rock highly conducive to the formation of thunder eggs. This is why we see so many variations from so many localities in the state. But no Oregon agate collecting site is as famous as Richardson Ranch, a privately owned ranch near Madras that produces thousands of specimens each year. The ranch encompasses several thunder egg-producing rock beds, which each yield distinct agate varieties. Some contain beautiful blue bands, others complex plume growths, but most contain some water-level banding. Due to their abundance, water-level agates from Richardson Ranch are not particularly valuable, but no collection is complete without one.

Richardson Ranch thunder egg
A particularly colorful example of a Richardson thunder egg

Eggs from the ranch Richardson Ranch has long operated a pay-to-dig service, allowing ambitious collectors a chance to find their own thunder eggs. The most desirable Richardson Ranch specimens are certainly those with blue fortification banding, very finely delineated water-level layering, or geode cavities containing interesting growths, but the odds are that you're more likely to find thunder eggs filled with moss and tube formations. These are the specimens typically considered "junk" by serious collectors, and many are sliced repeatedly in search of something more desirable. At area rock sales, these slices are often found in stacks or piled in buckets, often priced considerably lower than their finely banded counterparts. Though ignored by most collectors, these slices can actually be some of the most stunning examples of moss or tube agates in the United States once polished. They are often colorful, well-formed and translucent, so be open to collecting all varieties of thunder eggs. For a fraction of the price of a "good" agate, you can add many fantastic specimens to your shelf.

Round Mountain agates
This specimen shows characteristic coloration

Round Mountain agates

The area near Round Mountain, south of Duncan, Arizona, is a well-known locality for several varieties of agates. The primary types that attract collectors are fortification agates, plume agates, agate geodes and the rare fire agate. Water-level agates are possibly the least famous agates from the area, but Round Mountain's water-level agates are lovely, often colored in soft pastel shades of pink, grayish blue and peach, and they contain horizontal layers of varying thicknesses. The presence of water-level agates in an area with so many other different agate types is surprising when one considers that most theorists believe water-level agates formed in very wet, perhaps even tropical, conditions. For all of these varieties of agates to form at or near the same locality is unique, to say the least.

Spotted with color Always remember that unless an agate is white or colorless, it contains inclusions. Iron minerals, such as hematite, are the primary colorants in agates, but there can be other impurities as well. Most of the time, these impurities are microscopic, but occasionally agates will exhibit impurities large enough to be visible as a tiny fleck or spot of color in the chalcedony. When many of these little growths are present in an agate, it can give the stone an interesting speckled appearance. The agates from Round Mountain, Arizona, are often particularly good examples of this trait, containing dots of inclusions along the boundaries of their bands.

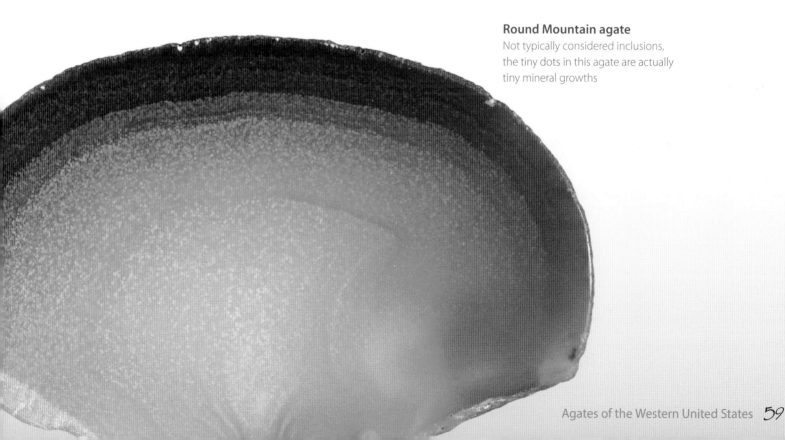

Round Mountain agate
Not typically considered inclusions, the tiny dots in this agate are actually tiny mineral growths

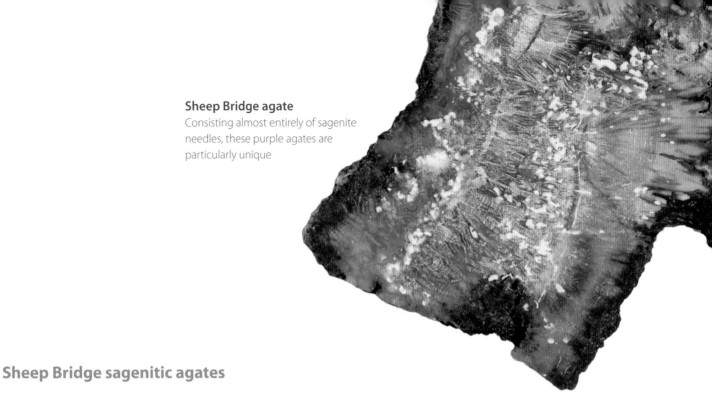

Sheep Bridge agate
Consisting almost entirely of sagenite needles, these purple agates are particularly unique

Sheep Bridge sagenitic agates

Northeast of Phoenix, Arizona, along the Verde River, is Sheep Bridge, a crossing once used by sheep herders but today only frequented by hikers. This remote area hosts a few varieties of agates but none more peculiar than the locality's namesake Sheep Bridge sagenitic agates. These agates are unique not only for their characteristic purple color, but because they consist almost entirely of sagenitic growths. Most sagenitic agates formed "normally" but included growths of a few other minerals. Sheep Bridge agates, on the other hand, are surrounded on all sides by dozens of sagenitic growths with only a small section of banded agate at the center, if any at all. An unusual and beautiful addition to your collection, the lavender hues and white highlights of Sheep Bridge agates draw attention to the visible crystal structure of the inclusions, which appear to have originally been a mixture of calcite, barite and zeolite minerals.

Tavenier thunder egg agates

Tavenier thunder eggs, named for the owner of the mine that originally produced the agates, are found in New Mexico, just a short distance from the historic and very well-known Baker Ranch thunder egg locality. Not all, but most, Tavenier thunder eggs contain water-level banding, which is interesting because the nearby Baker Ranch agates yield very few water-level agates, suggesting that they formed at different times and in different climates, despite their proximity to each other. Though they're not a very well-known variety, many Tavenier eggs are very well formed and typically dark gray with reddish highlights, making them attractive additions to your collection.

Tavenier thunder egg
A characteristic example of a
Tavenier thunder egg

Teepee Canyon agates

Found just a few miles west of the area famous for Fairburn agates, Teepee Canyon agates are named for the hills from which they are mined. Though once more abundant than they are today, these South Dakota agates are still one of the most well-known and popular varieties from the midwestern United States, if not the entire country. Also known as "Hell's Canyon," the hot, dry Teepee Canyon area is thought to have produced its agates from the same geological activity that developed the Fairburn agates, and both varieties formed as pockets within limestone, a sedimentary rock. Other than that, the two kinds of agates are quite distinct; Teepee Canyon agates can be found in fairly large sizes, often still embedded in their host rock, and are surprisingly consistent in coloration. Virtually every specimen exhibits nearly identical shades of red, deep orange, yellow and white. In contrast, Fairburn agates are generally smaller, more weathered and smoothed, and occur in a rainbow of colors.

Teepee Canyon agate
Often large, Teepee Canyon agates are virtually always found within a mass of host rock

Agates with (beneficial) faults Teepee Canyon agates have become more expensive to purchase in recent years, and collecting them is difficult due to private or protected land in the area. In addition, most specimens are acquired by breaking them directly out of their solid host rock. Still, they are worth pursuing, not only for their beauty but because they are scientifically important, largely due to the large number of faults found within them. In an agate, faults form when a shift in the surrounding rock breaks the agate, creating a crack that is later "healed" with quartz or another material. Often the broken pieces changed position, sometimes dramatically, resulting in misaligned banding. Faults are more than just a simple break or crack; they provide a glimpse into an agate's geological history.

Teepee Canyon agates provide some of North America's best examples of faulted agates, with most specimens containing dozens of faults. In contrast, faults tend to be rare from other agate localities. Teepee agates are also vividly colored, and their reds, yellows and oranges contrast well with the faults, which are typically filled with white quartz. This makes them interesting pieces for scientists to study and for collectors to admire.

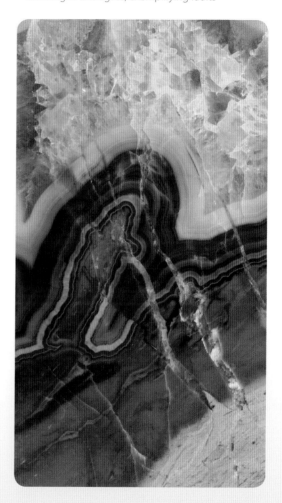

Teepee Canyon agate
Large quartz-filled cracks interrupt the banding of this agate, exemplifying faults

Texas plume agates
These examples exhibit the seemingly organic nature of plumes

Texas plume agates

There are dozens of well-known, popular varieties of agates from North America. But a few decades ago, fewer types were known and just a handful were king. Plume agates have long been favored, and many of the very best plumes were found in western Texas. Though there are several localities in the area that produce them, they are generally all lumped together simply as "Texas plume agates." Most of the stones contain dark-colored plumes surrounded by lighter chalcedony, and reddish specimens are especially valued, as well as those with particularly large and wild plumes that branch in all directions. In the past (and today, but to a lesser extent), Texas plume agates were cut thinly to reveal all of the different plume formations a specimen had to offer. Slices were then often trimmed further so that the result was a square, polished piece of agate containing a single fine plume, ready for use in jewelry.

Torpedo Bed thunder egg agates

The famous Baker Ranch thunder egg locality in New Mexico actually consists of several agate-producing beds of rock spread over a large area. Sometimes two or more nearby outcroppings of rock that each yield agates are actually different sides of the same rock formation. This is the case with Baker Ranch agates, and agates from each outcrop tend to have a different name, despite the fact that most of them formed at the same time and in the same body of rock. Torpedo Bed thunder eggs, named for an abundance of specimens with an elongated shape, are dug from a bed of rock south of the main Baker Ranch agate-producing site. Torpedo Bed agates typically have well-formed fortification patterns but don't share the typical Baker Ranch agate coloration, instead developing in a rainbow of colors. Unfortunately, they're difficult to come by, however, and don't turn up for sale very often.

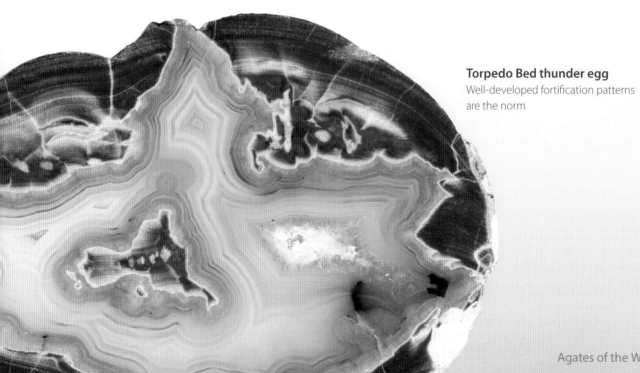

Torpedo Bed thunder egg
Well-developed fortification patterns are the norm

Trent sagenitic agates

As intricate and beautiful as sagenitic agates can be, there are few surprises when it comes to their coloration. It seems that no matter where the agate is from, most of the embedded crystals are rusty shades of brown, yellow, white or black. But not those from Trent, Oregon. The vein agates from this rural area set themselves apart with bright, vividly colored sagenite inclusions consisting of blood-red realgar crystals and yellow-orange streaks of orpiment and pararealgar, all of which are arsenic-bearing minerals. In some exceptional specimens, little silvery gray crystals of pure arsenic metal can even be found. Needless to say, these minerals are extremely rare in North America's agates, which makes these agates valuable and worthy of study. Though specimens from this unique occurrence are hard to come by today, they're instantly recognizable when you spot one.

Trent realgar sagenite
The blood-red realgar crystals make
Trent sagenitic agates like no other

Van Horn plume agate
This agate slice gives a unique view of the tops
of plume structures, rather than the sides

Van Horn plume agates

Western Texas is an agate-rich region where plume agates are abundant. While most are lumped together as "Texas plume agates," a few varieties stand out from the crowd, including the exquisite Van Horn plume agates. Named for the nearby town of Van Horn, specimens often consist entirely of plumes and contain little or no banding. The plume formations themselves are typically black or very dark brown and appear to "float" through nearly transparent colorless or gray chalcedony. The dark color of the plumes can likely be attributed to mineral compounds rich in manganese, instead of the more common iron-based plumes that appear red, yellow or brown in color. While they can still be collected, your best bet for adding one to your collection is at a rock sale, where, like many plume agates, they are often sold as cut slices.

Washington carnelian agates

The term carnelian originated centuries ago as a name for intense reddish orange translucent chalcedony. Today, the definition has been extended to agates, but sometimes a bit too liberally, as much of what is called "carnelian" today is not of the true, intense carnelian coloration. But that isn't the case with Washington's carnelian agates, found in several areas in the western portion of the state, particularly near Mount Rainier. Though many are not well banded and others are found broken or have a large core of quartz, their stunningly bright color makes up for these shortcomings. For years, they have been a popular variety and rewarding discovery for rock hounds.

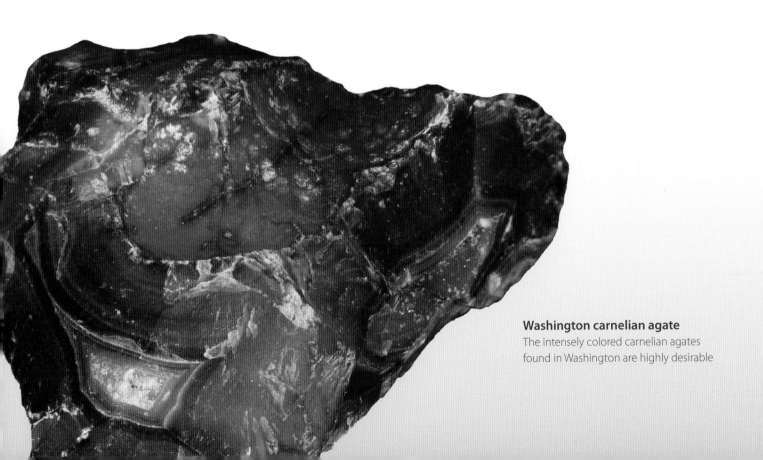

Washington carnelian agate
The intensely colored carnelian agates found in Washington are highly desirable

Wingate Pass agate
Red, mineral-rich plumes fill this rare
specimen of Death Valley plume agate

Wingate Pass agates

Death Valley, in the Mojave Desert of southeast California, is infamous as the site of the hottest air temperature ever recorded (134 degrees Fahrenheit, if you were wondering), but the area has also yielded more than a few agates. Wingate Pass, just southwest of Death Valley itself, is home to some of the most interesting and vividly colored plume agates in all of the United States. Going by the names "Wingate Pass agates" or "Death Valley plume agates," depending on whom you ask, these beautiful specimens are typically flame-red to orange in color, as if to mimic the heat of the area that produces them. Unfortunately, the original site of the Wingate Pass agates as well as numerous nearby agate-producing locations are now part of an expansive military training area and entering the territory is prohibited. But if you're lucky, you may come across a dealer with a specimen or two that was obtained before the military base was established.

Agates
of the Eastern United States

The eastern half of the United States cannot boast the impressive number of varieties native to the western half of the country, but what it lacks in quantity it makes up for in quality. Many rare, unique and scientifically important agate varieties are found here, including some of the world's oldest agates—those from the Lake Superior area. The best of what this region has to offer is shown here, and these agates represent some of the most historically significant varieties in the country.

Lake Superior agate
Some of the continent's finest fortification agates come from the Lake Superior region

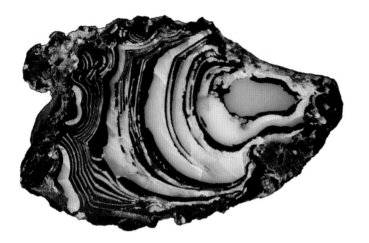

Copper replacement agate
Intricate bands of pure copper make this tiny,
1-inch agate worth hundreds of dollars

Copper replacement agate
A copper eye, as in this specimen, is an exceptionally rare find

Copper replacement agates

Of all the world's agates that contain inclusions, Michigan's copper replacement agates are easily one of the most spectacular varieties. Jutting into the southern side of Lake Superior is the Keweenaw Peninsula, which is the heart of the area known locally as "copper country." As the site of one of the world's largest and most important copper deposits, the entire peninsula was mined extensively for decades, and likely will be again someday. But the mining didn't only bring copper up from the depths of the earth; all manner of beautiful, rare minerals were produced. Today, at the sites of the old, abandoned mines, there are enormous piles of unwanted rock, which was removed from the mines long ago. Known as mine dumps, waste rock or overburden piles, these mountains of broken boulders still contain collectibles, including copper and, of course, agates. And a rare few of the piles hide small agates containing entire bands composed of solid copper.

Michigan's metallic mystery Copper replacement agates are one of the great enigmas in the agate world. We don't fully understand how regular agates form, let alone agates with copper banding. But it is hypothesized that these agates originally formed with highly impure bands composed of soft minerals, particularly calcite, which alternated with hard, tan-colored chalcedony bands. Later, volcanic waters dissolved the soft, impure layers and left copper in their place. However they came to be, their presence in only a few mine dumps tells us that they are not a widespread variety and didn't form in all copper-bearing rock formations. When found, copper replacement agates don't look like agates at all. Instead, they are found as small nodules (ball-like growths) still embedded in their host basalt and are coated with chlorite, a soft, greasy-looking dark green mineral. This coating disguises the agates, making them look identical to nodules of other minerals until cut open.

Copper replacement agates with eyes attract the most attention. Because these agates are found as whole nodules, most must be sawn in half; sawing through an eye gives it the appearance of being a "half-eye," or an eye viewed in cross-section. A whole eye is far more desirable, of course, but finding such an agate is a matter of chance or very careful polishing by a professional.

Copper replacement agate
The rarity of these agates makes them legendary among North American collectors

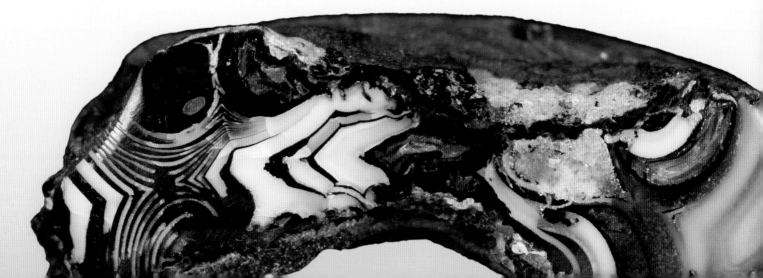

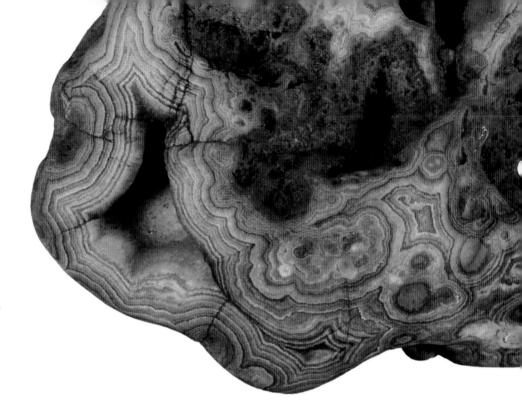

Crowley Ridge agates

The southeastern portion of the United States is not home to a large variety of agates; compared to the agate-rich western states, the southeast can seem almost barren. But Arkansas does produce Crowley Ridge agates, which are, without question, one of the nation's most famous agate varieties. Originating from the landmark of the same name in northeastern Arkansas, Crowley Ridge agates are found all over the region, as they were moved by water to nearby states and are even found as far south as Louisiana and the Gulf of Mexico. (In fact, most "Louisiana agates" on the market are actually Crowley Ridge agates.) The majority of specimens are found in unremarkable shades of yellow or brown, but a small percentage exhibit the most desirable coloration of Crowley Ridge agates: deep, rich shades of red, with dark brown and purple highlights. These colors are noteworthy because they were not originally present in the agates but rather developed later as a result of the agates being naturally heated, particularly by wildfires "roasting" their color-causing impurities.

Beware of flame-broiled agates Crowley Ridge agates are virtually always weathered until rounded and smoothed, and specimens can be found up to a foot in size. Even average samples show beautiful, almost lace-like banding, which is desirable in any color, but when a finely patterned specimen is red, its value can increase tenfold. For this reason, one must be wary when purchasing Crowley Ridge agates. Because these agates owe their coloration to being heated—primarily by wildfires—some collectors have been able to replicate the coloration by putting common yellow specimens in a very hot oven, changing the coloration to the more valuable reddish hues. Sometimes this is done just out of curiosity, but all too often unscrupulous dealers try to sell them as genuine.

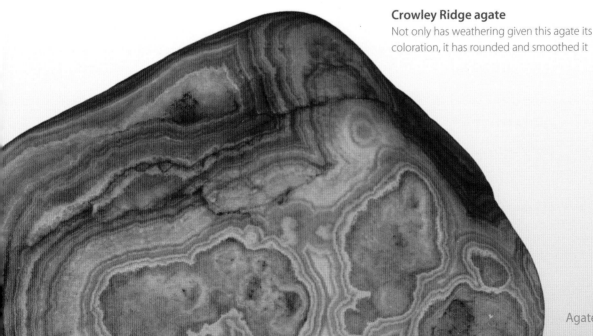

Crowley Ridge agate
Not only has weathering given this agate its coloration, it has rounded and smoothed it

Tips to identify treated Crowley Ridge agates When Crowley Ridge agates are unnaturally heated, it is referred to as "heat treating." There are two ways to identify a heat-treated agate. First, red Crowley Ridge agates are rare, so if the dealer has many for sale at prices that seem too good to be true, you should be suspicious. And second, wildfires presumably don't heat the agates evenly, often resulting in just portions of an agate being reddish, whereas "cooked" agates are too perfect and typically uniformly colored.

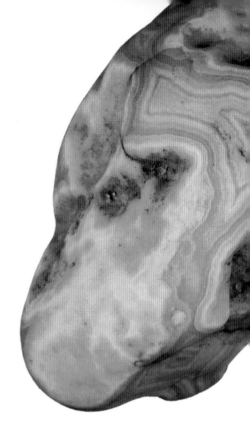

Crowley Ridge agates
These specimens represent coloration before and after natural "roasting," with the altered agate being the one with more orange and red hues

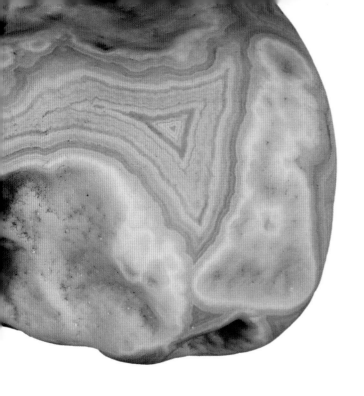

Smooth and sculpted Crowley Ridge agates are sedimentary in nature, and over the years wind, water and ice have turned their soft host rock to dust. For this reason, these agates are virtually always found loose with no attached rock. And although agates are extremely hard, such weathering does not leave them unscathed. The same forces that freed them from their host rock also rounded them. In fact, the vast majority of Crowley Ridge agates exhibit few rough surfaces or sharp angular edges (unless recently broken, of course); as most other North American agates have some rough surfaces, this makes Crowley Ridge agates unique. Because they are smoothed and sculpted, these agates are very popular with collectors. Aside from the flowing water and wind-blown particles that shaped the agates, the most interesting weathering undergone by Crowley Ridge agates is the aforementioned change in coloration caused by natural heating. The reddish hues are thought to be the result of wildfires in the region "roasting" the color-causing impurities and starting a chemical reaction.

Crowley Ridge agatized coral

At the same mines famous for Arkansas' Crowley Ridge agates, collectors find weathered pieces of fossilized coral that consist almost entirely of chalcedony. Though called "agatized coral," these specimens, by definition, are not agates, but share so many properties with true agates that the name continues to stick. Identified by their segmented, gauze-like surface texture, corals replaced by chalcedony are found in many places, but the rounded, smoothed pebbles from Crowley Ridge are among the most attractive.

Crowley Ridge coral
While not actually agate, these specimens and their gauze-like texture are found alongside Crowley Ridge agates

Kentucky agates
These agates, from Estill County, Kentucky, show the common and desirable mustard-yellow coloration

Kentucky agates

"Kentucky agates," as general as that name may be, are Kentucky's claim to agate fame and the state's gemstone since 2000. They're found in various rock outcrops and rivers in several counties, but since most are believed to have originated from a similar source, they tend to be lumped together under one name. Formed in limestone within round pockets thought to have originally been occupied by fossils, Kentucky agates are almost always found loose and don't show much banding until cut. But when these agates are cut open, collectors are rewarded with a stunning array of rich coloration, from intense yellows and oranges to muted pinks and blues. The most valuable Kentucky agates, the ones that collectors from all over the world strive to obtain, are those that are nearly black with tomato-red bands. Such specimens are easily some of the most expensive agates in the entire Southeast.

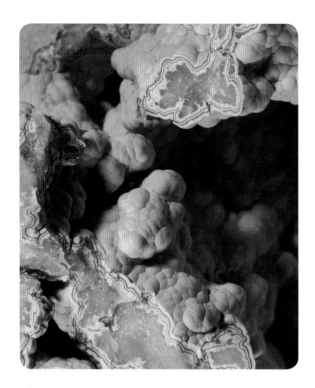

Keswick agate
This close-up shows just a few of the banded botryoidal formations at the center of a massive 49-pound specimen

Keswick agates

Iowa is famous worldwide for the crystal-filled geodes produced near the city of Keokuk, but northwest of that lauded locality is Keswick, a community with a quarry of the same name that yields the most sought after agates in the state. Keswick agates are sedimentary in nature and formed within nodules, or round masses, of chert, a sedimentary rock composed of microscopic quartz grains. Filling cavities in the rock, these agates are unique in that they are mostly pale and are often white or cream-colored with shades of yellow, but with sparse beautifully contrasting bands of bright flame-orange or red. The larger specimens are most interesting and are generally hollow geodes that don't always resemble typical agates. Sometimes measuring a foot or more across, large Keswick agates predominantly feature botryoidal, or grape-like, growths of white chalcedony within the cavity. These lumpy formations contain banding within, which is most often revealed, unfortunately, when quarrying equipment breaks up the agates.

Lake Superior agate
Even large agates from the region are polished on one side to improve the visibility of their banding

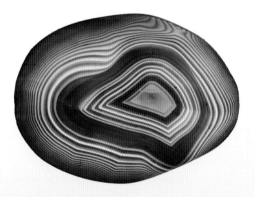

Lake Superior agate
Some of North America's priciest agates are red-and-white Lake Superior fortification agates

Lake Superior agates

At more than one billion years in age, the agates from the Lake Superior region in Minnesota, Wisconsin, Michigan and Ontario are among the oldest agates in the world. They grew within gas bubbles that were trapped in basalt, then spent an eternity buried beneath thousands of feet of rock. The most arduous period of their lives was yet to come when the glaciers of the ice ages scoured the region. Through all this, the agates endured and eventually were scattered all over the region, before finally being buried once more in loose gravel. But their incredible age has taken its toll, and finding a laker with no noticeable cracks or damage is next to impossible. Similarly, it's rare to find agates larger than an inch or two because the glaciers wore so much material away.

Lakers, as they are called locally, are known and valued for many of their features, such as their wide variation in color and glacially smoothed exteriors, to name a few. Their often well-developed and wildly banded fortification patterns are most significant. Few exhibit idealized circular, ring-like banding, and the chalcedony layers must instead contort and twist around abundant mineral inclusions or irregularities in the agate's shape. A core of coarsely crystallized quartz very often lies at the center of a Lake Superior agate, but the most desirable specimens are "solid" agates consisting entirely of banded chalcedony.

Lake Superior agate
Water-level agates are common from Lake Superior

Lake Superior water-level agates

The Lake Superior region is renowned for its fortification agates, but water-level agates are abundant as well. This is a little unusual —most regions usually only produce either fortification agates or water-level agates, as they form under very different conditions. The fact that both types are common implies that some dramatic changes in climate and geology were occurring when they formed. Aside from their horizontal banding, however, Lake Superior's water-level agates share most of their features with the rest of the region's agates, including their predominantly brownish red coloration and glacially smoothed outer surfaces.

An enduring mystery Like other areas with water-level agates, specimens from Lake Superior show varying amounts of horizontal layering. Some have just a few layers at the bottom of the agate while others consist entirely of water-level bands. The majority are somewhere in the middle, with the upper portion of the agate containing fortification banding and, more commonly, coarse quartz. Some specimens are especially interesting (and bewildering), featuring bands that change color and texture along their length, giving portions of the agates' horizontal banding an uneven, splotchy appearance. This unexplained phenomenon isn't unique to Lake Superior's agates, but the region produces many specimens that will likely be useful for future study.

Lake Superior agate
It is very typical for a Lake Superior water-level agate to contain an upper section of quartz crystals

Lake Superior agate
This is a typical eye agate specimen from the region

Lake Superior eye agates

Eye agates can be found all over the continent, but few North American localities produce eye agates like those found near Lake Superior. The region's agates are known worldwide for exhibiting well-developed eye-like spots. Lake Superior agate eyes can vary a great deal; some specimens have large eyes with brightly colored rings, like a bull's-eye, while others have clusters of dozens of small eyes.

Lake Superior's eye agates are renowned largely because the eyes are so easy to see; in other localities, eyes are obscured by a rough outer coating of thick chalcedony or external mineral growths. In the Lake Superior region, eons of weathering have worn away these features. Too much weathering, however, and the eyes are worn away completely, as they are only surface features.

Eye agate imposters Many collections are rife with Lake Superior "eye agates" that actually aren't eyes at all. It's easy for eager collectors to label any circular banded feature as an agate "eye" because eye agates are such desirable specimens. But as with any aspect of agate collecting, better familiarizing yourself with true agate eyes will help determine if you actually have one. Agate eyes are hemispheres, or half-spheres, which grow inward from the outer edges of an agate, and few grow much larger than a quarter of an inch. Under magnification, eyes exhibit tiny chalcedony fibers that radiate outward from a central point. Large, not-quite-perfectly circular banded patterns closer to the center of an agate are more likely the result of inclusions called tubes or, very often, are merely bands that happen to resemble eyes. Though it isn't difficult to tell a genuine eye from a look-alike, misidentifications continue to occur thanks to how valuable Lake Superior eye agates are.

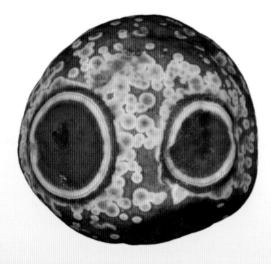

Lake Superior agate
Two large eyes among dozens
of smaller ones

Lake Superior moss agates

Moss agates are ubiquitous in the Lake Superior region, much to the chagrin of local collectors, who seek the area's more valuable fortification agates. Moss agates, on the other hand, are typically viewed as valueless. Most prolific collectors have hundreds, if not thousands, of discarded moss agates tossed aside into piles or buckets. But if they would take the time to cut and polish them, they would be rewarded with not only some of the oldest moss agates in North America, but some of the most compelling. Richly colored in iron-rich shades of red and brown, Lake Superior's moss agates are often so weathered and altered that they reveal features not seen in other North American specimens, making them worth the trouble that only a few collectors afford them.

Lake Superior agate
Commonly considered "junk," moss agates like this one can be gorgeous when polished

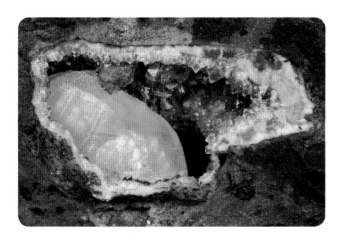

Lake Superior agate
A large calcite crystal hiding in an agate geode (specimen courtesy of Chris Cordes)

Lake Superior agate geodes

Though there are dozens of variations of Lake Superior agates, they don't often turn up as geodes. Most consist entirely of chalcedony banding or have a core of solid quartz, but only a small percentage are hollow. Maybe there were more Lake Superior agate geodes long ago, but the crushing weight of the glaciers that scoured the region as recently as 10,000 years ago likely smashed most of them, leaving only a lucky few behind. Others survive today because they're still embedded in their host rock. Whatever the case, a few Lake Superior agate geodes hold amazing mineral growths, some of which are almost unheard of at other localities in North America. Most local collectors see agate geodes as a curiosity, but considering the age of the agates and all that they've endured, they should be seen as a wonder of the natural world.

Sagenitic agates from Lake Superior

All of Lake Superior's agates are full of mineral inclusions. Nearly every specimen has some kind of crystal or mineral formation embedded within it, most of the time in the form of unremarkable, irregular growths on its outer edges. But the sagenitic agates from the area, especially those from northern Minnesota, are an exception and are widely viewed as some of the finest examples of agates containing inclusions in all of North America. Lake Superior's sagenitic agates exhibit stunning ray-like circular arrangements of crystals. These formed due to the presence of a number of minerals, but especially because of members of the zeolite group, minerals that form in volcanic rocks as groundwater interacts with them. Many zeolites form as slender, needle-like crystals grouped into clusters that grow outward from a single point. As these formations competed for space in a vesicle (gas bubble) that was also home to a developing agate, the delicate crystals were encased in the much harder chalcedony, thereby becoming an inclusion.

Lake Superior's agates sometimes contain sagenite formations large enough to dominate an entire specimen. When well developed, these are the most sought after sagenites, particularly by collectors of "weird" agates. Other specimens have hollow sagenite needles, brightly colored staining, or are broken and show a different view of the sagenite formation.

Lake Superior agate
Coarse sagenite needles extend nearly the full length of this agate

Lake Superior agate
A billion years of weathering have given this sagenitic agate unique features and colors

Tube agates from Lake Superior

Most of Lake Superior's many agate varieties are a result of the mineral inclusions embedded within them. It's hard to know the exact conditions in which these ancient agates formed, but they were clearly conducive to the formation of many other minerals as well, and Lake Superior's tube agates are evidence of this. As their name implies, tube agates contain banded tunnel-like structures, which are sometimes filled with chalcedony or are hollow. Tubes typically developed around needle- or pendant-like formations and crystals of other minerals that were then coated with layer after layer of chalcedony as the agate developed around them. Later, acidic water dissolved the tube-forming minerals in many agates, leaving hollow channels that were often later filled with quartz or chalcedony. The result are tube agates, with "worms" of chalcedony burrowing through them, often visible as eye-like rings on one side that extend through the center to the other side.

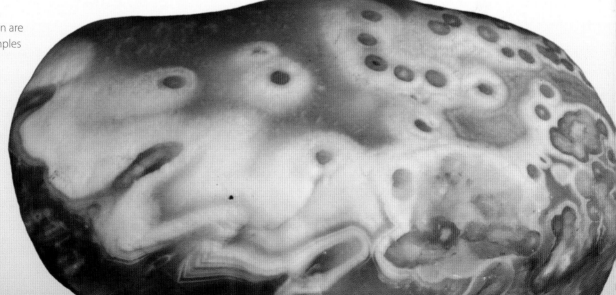

Lake Superior agate
Tube agates from the region are not rare, but very fine examples are (specimen courtesy of Terry Roses)

Lake Superior agate
This is a perfect and highly valuable example of a "water-washed" agate

Water-washed agates from Lake Superior

When an agate is cracked, worn, broken and otherwise weathered, its value typically isn't enhanced. But the opposite is true of the Lake Superior region's "water-washed" agates. Because they underwent a great deal of weathering, these agates exhibit no rough surfaces, hard edges or sharp corners, and while this has also worn the agates down to a smaller size, many Lake Superior collectors prize fine water-washed agates over all others. Of course, it wasn't water alone that rounded and smoothed these agates; it took eons of being rolled along river bottoms and pushed and pulled through gravel by waves. The glaciers of the last ice age played a large role, too. As the region's agates were scraped up by the massive ice sheets, they were trapped beneath, along with billions of tons of gravel and pulverized rock that ground the agates down.

Lake Superior agate
Three views of the same water-washed agate
illustrate how every side is beautifully banded

Beauty from any angle Most Lake Superior agates exhibit some surfaces that are
smoothed and worn—they've been around for over one billion years, after all—but few
qualify for the title of "water-washed." This exclusive label is given only to those agates
that are shaped like the entirely rounded stones typically found on the shore. But why
do local collectors find this characteristic so desirable? Simply put, a high quality water-
washed agate is all banding, encircled with color. There are no rough, thick exteriors to
obscure the pattern, and no corners or edges to make the shape of a specimen irregular.
They are considered the most aesthetically pleasing Lake Superior agates, as they show
their beauty from all sides and from any angle. But their value is as legendary as their
appearance; even small specimens can be remarkably valuable, and some extraordinary
examples have been known to fetch thousands of dollars.

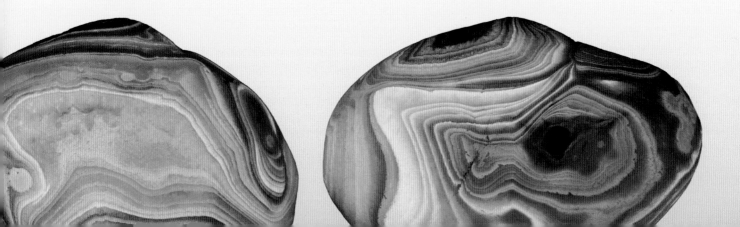

Minnesota sedimentary agate
The cavity this agate formed in was
originally created by ancient bacteria
(specimen courtesy of Phil Burgess)

Minnesota sedimentary agates

Minnesota is best known for Lake Superior agates, but those aren't the
only agates in the state. In the southeast, unique sedimentary agates
can be found that formed as a replacement of stromatolites, which are
rounded colonies of bacteria that form in shallow seas. Full of cavities
and rough, ragged edges, these agates are found in limestone intergrown
with chert, a silica-rich sedimentary rock, all of which combine to give
us a glimpse of Minnesota's marine past.

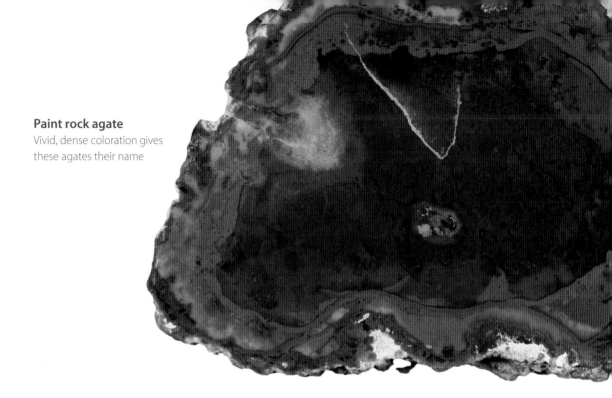

Paint rock agate
Vivid, dense coloration gives these agates their name

Paint rock agates

The Cumberland Plateau is a large elevated region consisting of weathered hills just west of the Appalachian Mountains. It stretches across several southeastern states, but agates turn up where it crosses the border between Alabama and Tennessee. Paint rock agates are fairly rare and very colorful, and they get their name because their coloration is so dense and opaque that it appears as if it were painted onto the stones. Typically collected loose in rivers, freed from their host limestone, the best specimens have complete patterns of wavy, ribbon-like bands and amazing deep orange-red, mustard yellow or greenish blue colors. Like many of the region's agates, however, paint rock agates are found on land that is now privately owned.

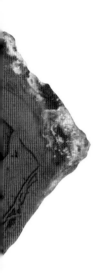

Tampa Bay agatized coral

As a state that is comprised of soft sedimentary rocks overlain by sand, Florida is not very geologically diverse; it certainly isn't the first state to come to mind when the subject is agates. But one very famous variety of agate is found near Tampa Bay, and the form these agates take is even more peculiar than their presence in the Sunshine State. Called Tampa Bay agatized coral, these agates developed in cavities made by ancient coral and their external surfaces perfectly illustrate this fact, as they exhibit the well-preserved features of the coral's structure. When cut open, however, a hollow cavity ringed with banded agate is found inside. Their coloration is typically grayish blue or brown, rarely red, but a lifetime of tropical weather has leached some specimens of their color, turning parts of them white. Popular since the early 1800s, Tampa Bay's agates are certainly some of the most compelling finds in all of North America.

Tampa Bay agate
This rare agate formed within a cavity made by ancient coral

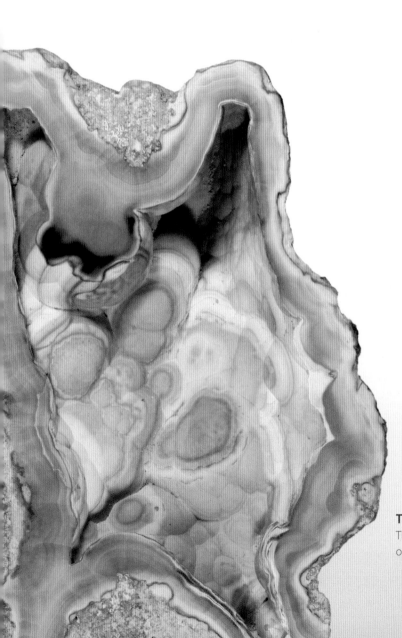

A record of ancient life Though it is part of their common name, calling the Tampa Bay specimens "agatized coral" is misleading. The term "agatized" is typically reserved for organic material that has been replaced by chalcedony cell-by-cell through the process of fossilization, but this was not the case in Tampa Bay agates. It is more accurate to call them pseudomorphs. A pseudomorph is a mineral formation that takes the shape of another, either by a slow chemical transformation of the original mineral or when a mineral fills a cavity made by another mineral. The Tampa Bay agates are an example of the latter, and formed when coral that was encased in rock dissolved, leaving coral-shaped cavities behind. As silica derived from ocean sediments seeped into these cavities, chalcedony bands formed, creating the agates for which Florida is so famous.

Tampa Bay agatized coral
This cut pair shows the beautiful patterns only revealed when specimens are cut open

A rare find Unfortunately for collectors, specimens can be hard to come by, as the areas in which they were once found are now protected or covered by urban development.

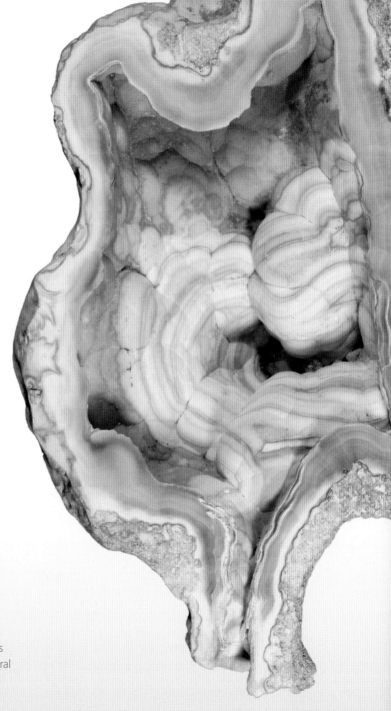

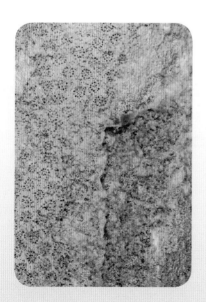

Tampa Bay agatized coral
The exterior of a specimen shows
intricate details of the original coral

Wisconsin thunder egg
White clay-filled cracks and pits are
indicators of this agate's difficult past

Wisconsin thunder egg agates

The overwhelming majority of thunder egg agates in North America come from the west,
but a recent discovery has unearthed peculiar specimens from northern Wisconsin. Along
with a few other exceptions from Minnesota, Michigan and Québec, these are some of the
only thunder eggs found in the eastern half of the continent. Unfortunately, because of their
rarity, their exact location has largely been kept secret by the landowner. Still, this rarity makes
them interesting to geologists as well as to thunder egg collectors. These thunder eggs have
clearly been through a lot, as most are highly weathered, and though not all specimens
contain banded chalcedony, those that do tend to exhibit bands in shades of tan, gray and
white, likely the result of their original colors being washed away by acidic groundwater. They
are also typically fractured, with many large cracks that filled in with white clay formed during
the decay of their host rock. Given their appearance, Wisconsin's thunder eggs have no doubt
had a difficult existence.

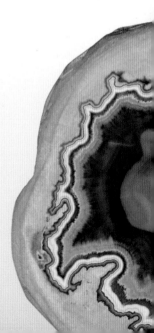

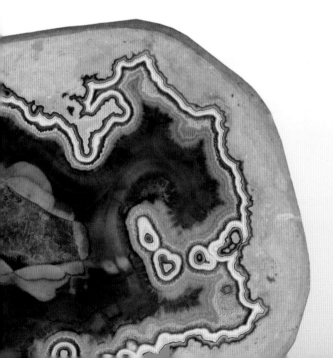

Union Road agate
Strong bands and a hollow center
are common features

Union Road agates

Union Road agates are perhaps North America's best example of
an agate variety that can no longer be collected. Unlike other agate
varieties, they aren't inaccessible because of issues with private land
or legal battles among landowners, but because the collecting site
essentially no longer exists. These agates' interesting story begins
in the 1950s during the construction of Interstate 55, just south of
St. Louis, Missouri, when digging equipment unearthed concretions within the limestone. Concretions are hard, round masses
of material that develop within rock; they typically contain nothing of interest. But a small percentage of the concretions found at
the junction of I-55 and I-270 contained banded agates, and local
collectors quickly began hoarding as many as they could. Soon
after, the highway was completed and the deposit of concretions
was covered over. Today, the surrounding area is a dense residential
neighborhood, and a shopping mall covers the site of the discovery.
The only evidence remaining is the nondescript city road for which
the agates are named.

A sedimentary type of agate, Union Road agates were easily freed
from their soft host rock by the nearby Mississippi River. The river
also "washed" their coloration, making many specimens muted and
unevenly colored. But it isn't a detriment; instead, it makes them
even more unique. And due to their finite number and great rarity,
even an average specimen is desirable.

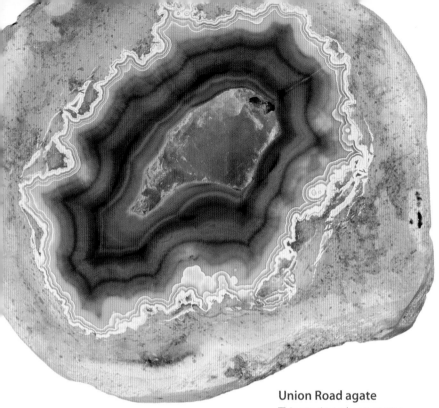

Union Road agate
This specimen has a center
completely filled with calcite

Geodes from Union Road It's worth mentioning that despite the fact that Union Road agates primarily exhibit fortification patterns, they are also frequently hollow geodes. There is little uniformity in cavity size from specimen to specimen; there are just as many agates with large central voids as there are small ones, but nearly all Union Road agate geodes are lined with countless tiny, transparent quartz crystals. A few house large calcite crystals, and rarely some have even been found to contain minute amounts of black hydrocarbons, such as bitumen (asphalt). When surrounded by agate bands that are often beautifully tinted with strange wavy, swirled blotches of color, these rare sedimentary agates from a now-built-over locality are some of the most beautiful and unique agate geodes in North America.

Union Road agate
A large percentage of
these agates are geodes

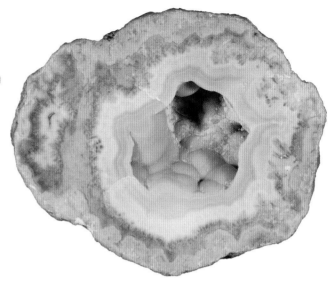

White ringer agate
These interesting agates have a surprising lack of color-causing impurities

White ringer agates

A number of quarries along the Mississippi River in Illinois and Iowa produce all kinds of interesting mineral formations, particularly geodes. Most of the geodes in the area are round, light-colored balls of rock weathered out of limestone. And when cut open, most are hollow with a lining of crystals. But white ringer agates, found near Warsaw, Illinois, contain banded chalcedony. They get their descriptive name from the way their characteristic white banding wraps around the perimeter of the agate. Each specimen typically only has a small amount of banding, and it often resembles a white ring around the center of the agate. The center, which is generally hollow, is often lined with well-developed quartz crystals, which results in beautiful, light-colored agate geodes that are popular among local collectors.

Michipicoten Island agate
Found at the bottom of Lake Superior,
these agates are a remote discovery

Agates
of Canada

From the lakes of British Columbia to the shores of Nova Scotia, Canada

is dotted with agate localities. Extremely rare agates, like those from

Michipicoten Island, and obscure varieties, such as those from Monte

Lake, are the norm for Canada. But it would seem that the Great White

North is home to far fewer agates than the United States, despite its greater

size. In reality, Canada is no doubt loaded with agates, but the vast amount

of unpopulated land means that possibly hundreds of localities are still

waiting to be discovered.

Michipicoten Island agates

Located on the eastern side of Lake Superior, uninhabited Michipicoten Island is ten miles from the mainland at its closest point. It is also the site of some of Canada's most elusive agates. Michipicoten Island's agates formed during the same geological events that created Lake Superior's famous agates on the western and southern shores of the big lake. But Michipicoten Island's agates tend to be colored in unique shades of pink, purple and red, seldom seen elsewhere around Lake Superior. They also often contain large mineral inclusions, such as crystals of calcite or masses of soft chlorite. Collecting is now prohibited on the remote island, but years ago adventurous divers off the coast were able to free Michipicoten Island agates from their host rock underwater. Though the most desirable specimens contain uninterrupted banding, the examples containing inclusions are often more interesting (and more affordable) for those who appreciate "strange" agates.

Michipicoten Island agate
Large masses of calcite mar the beautiful banding of this rare agate but are interesting as well

Mont Lyall thunder egg

Rare and unusual, these thunder eggs are sometimes hollow and, like this one, sometimes contain calcite

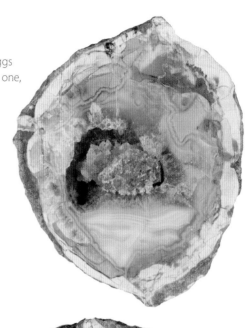

Mont Lyall thunder egg agates

When it comes to North American thunder eggs, the western United States and Mexico are the primary collecting destinations. Virtually every major variety of thunder egg comes from those volcanic areas, which is why it's particularly surprising to discover one type that originates in Canada—in Québec, no less. Hailing from a quarry in Mont Lyall, an area near the mouth of the St. Lawrence Seaway, Québec's thunder eggs are a rare find from a quarry that is now closed to collecting. Clearly older than most of the United States' thunder eggs, Mont Lyall eggs are all highly damaged, with numerous fractures and pale, bleached pink, orange and white coloration. Many are hollow and contain crudely formed quartz or calcite within the ragged geode cavity. By all accounts, these thunder eggs would not be especially noteworthy were it not for their unique and rare location, which makes them highly desired among thunder egg collectors.

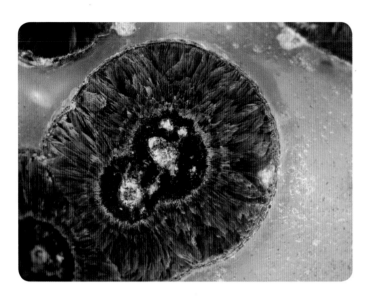

Monte Lake agate
Almost eye-like in appearance, Monte Lake sagenites are rare and exciting

Monte Lake agates

Monte Lake, a small body of water southeast of Kamloops, British Columbia, is the source of some interesting little agates. Though only loosely defined as agates, since they contain virtually no banding, the specimens from the lake are rounded bluish gray nodules dotted with brown or green sagenite formations. The sagenite growths are often so perfectly circular that they are frequently mislabeled as "eye agates" by sellers, but that's not to say that they often come up for sale. Information on the exact locality is sparse as well, and it appears that the local collectors prefer to keep it that way. Monte Lake agates may typically only measure an inch or two in size, but with beautifully intricate, fibrous sagenitic formations, they are certainly worth adding to your collection —if you can manage to find one.

Two Islands agates

In all of eastern Canada, one region is most famous for agates: the Bay of Fundy. The large Atlantic inlet separates New Brunswick from Nova Scotia, but it is the Nova Scotia side that produces many of the most interesting examples. The area of Two Islands, named for—what else?—two nearby islands, yields veins of agate still embedded in its host rock, though much of what local collectors call "agate" is actually colorful jasper. But true agate veins can be found here, sometimes within the jasper itself, and they are often light in color and delicately banded. Many of the agates from the Two Islands area of Nova Scotia are called "sea agates," a regional name for agates found on the coasts. While not as widely desirable or valuable as many of Nova Scotia's more "normal" varieties of agate, Two Islands agates are certainly an interesting and hard-to-find addition to your collection.

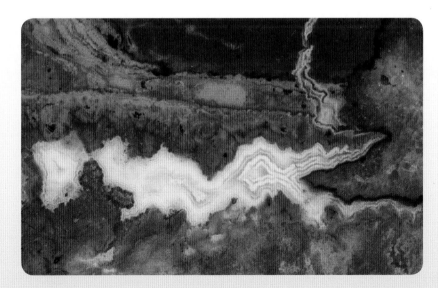

Two Islands agate
A white agate vein within jasper, which itself formed as a vein within rock

Thunder Bay agates

East of Thunder Bay, Ontario, on the northern edge of Lake Superior, a formation of limestone managed to survive the glaciers of the last ice age. This formation contains veins of agate, some several feet in length. Known as Thunder Bay agates, they are the only agates in the Lake Superior region that formed in a sedimentary rock environment. Generally colored in distinctive pale shades of yellow, orange and rust-red, they are impure and rich with mineral inclusions, particularly calcite, and very rarely can be found as stalactites, or icicle-like agate structures that hang from the roof of a cavity. Though a few extraordinary specimens were carried by the glaciers and have been found elsewhere, the majority of Thunder Bay agates are found still embedded in their host rock, which is, unfortunately, on private land now closed to collectors. Specimens don't often come up for sale, but hopefully collecting will again be allowed someday at the locality.

Thunder Bay agate
Typical structure and appearance, including ample quartz crystals

Thunder Bay agate
Bright orange coloration is most
desired but atypical of this agate type

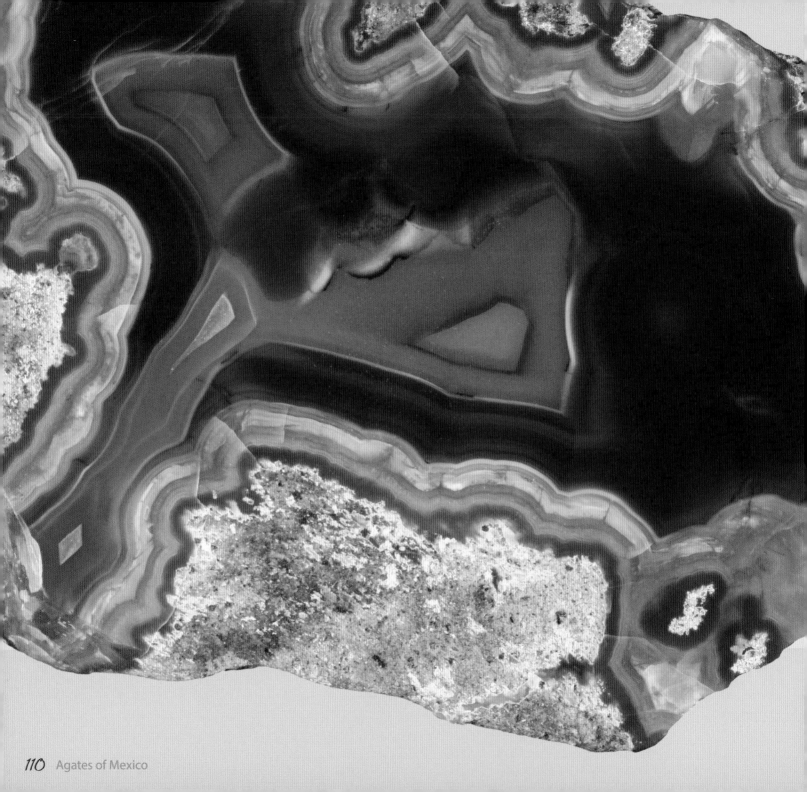

Laguna agate
Found in museums worldwide, some of
North America's best agates are lagunas

Agates
of Mexico

The indisputable kings of color, Mexico's agates are easily North America's

most vivid agates and are among the most valuable specimens as a result.

In addition, most of the country's agates are much younger than those

found in the United States and Canada, so many are damage-free and make

truly stunning specimens for your collection. With world-famous varieties

like laguna agates and century-old favorites like crazy lace, Mexico is a

spotlight region for North America's agates, and here we will discuss some

of the best agate types it has to offer.

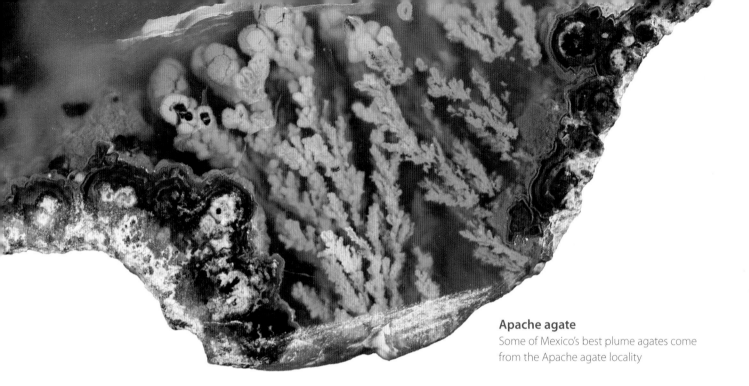

Apache agate
Some of Mexico's best plume agates come from the Apache agate locality

Apache agates

Not many collectors have heard of Chihuahua, Mexico's, Apache agates. That's partly because they haven't been mined since the 1960s, with the exception of some recent exploratory digs. Apache agates are named after the mine where they were first found. Most are fortification agates with richly colored red, brown and gray bands, but a small percentage contain plumes—rare formations that resemble tree branches or a column of smoke. There aren't a lot of plume-producing localities in Mexico, so beautiful examples of Apache agates often find their way into private collections and stay there.

Coyamito agates

Found not far from the famous laguna agate locality, Chihuahua, Mexico's, coyamito agates may not be quite as valuable as their cousins, but they are just as rare and famous. Named for the large cattle ranch on which they are mined, coyamito agates were once lumped together with laguna agates and other varieties from the area and exported en masse as "Mexican agates." Today they are rightfully given their own designation, and coyamitos have since become known for their variations in color. Virtually always cut in half and polished flat, and generally sold in pairs, coyamito agates are a favorite at rock shows. When looking through an assortment of them there is a good chance that you won't find any colored exactly alike. Rust-reds, yellows and bluish grays are common, but some of the rarer, more sought after colors include pinks, purples and even black, often in unique combinations.

Coyamito agate
As colorful as their cousins, the laguna agates, coyamito agates are highly desirable

A younger type of agate Like laguna agates, coyamito agates are young in comparison to other North American varieties. As they are younger, they've been subjected to less weathering, and their typically crack-free appearance reflects this. Many coyamito agates are geodes and have hollow centers lined with tiny quartz crystals or filled with calcite. Others contain inclusions of various minerals generally visible as embedded geometric masses. Though agate geodes and specimens with inclusions are certainly attractive to some collectors, they garner less attention than those that consist entirely of banded chalcedony, which are always considered more desirable and valuable. Access to the coyamito agate locality is severely limited, however, as the land is privately owned and exclusive mining rights are held only by one company.

Coyamito agates
The variations in color from specimen-to-specimen are often striking

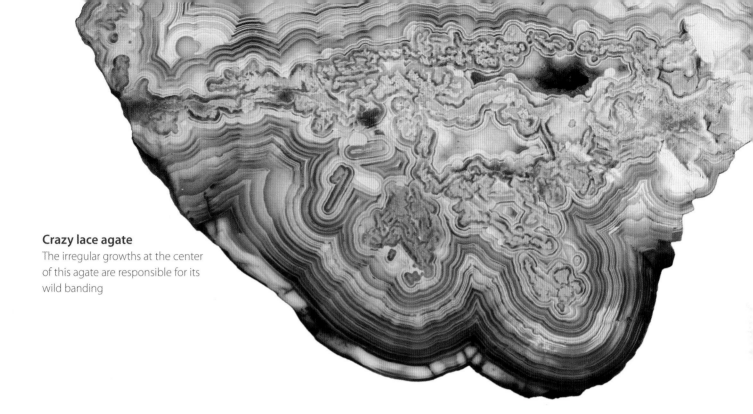

Crazy lace agate
The irregular growths at the center of this agate are responsible for its wild banding

Crazy lace agates

Mined in large quantities for decades, crazy lace agates are the most popular and widely known vein agates in North America. Found near Chihuahua, Mexico, their name may seem unusual and unscientific, but it is also apt, as the banding in a quality crazy lace agate specimen is wild and tangled but has a delicate order, like lace. Because of its dense, tightly layered banding and prices that are typically quite affordable, collectors have found crazy lace particularly attractive for lapidary use for many years. Case in point: when attending a rock sale, there is a good chance that you will find crazy lace agates, but in the form of cut slices or small polished pieces rather than as whole, natural specimens. Crazy lace agates are found in large masses with a great deal of banding, and slicing a large chunk of crazy lace agate yields dozens of beautiful pieces, each with a different pattern than the last.

Crazy patterns and a crazy number of inclusions Crazy lace agates formed within cracks and faults in limestone that originated from sediment on an ancient seafloor. As with many other kinds of sedimentary vein agates, crazy lace agates contain large amounts of mineral inclusions; in fact, these agates largely owe their namesake patterning to the inclusions trapped within them. As crazy lace agates formed, their banding had to accommodate countless existing mineral growths

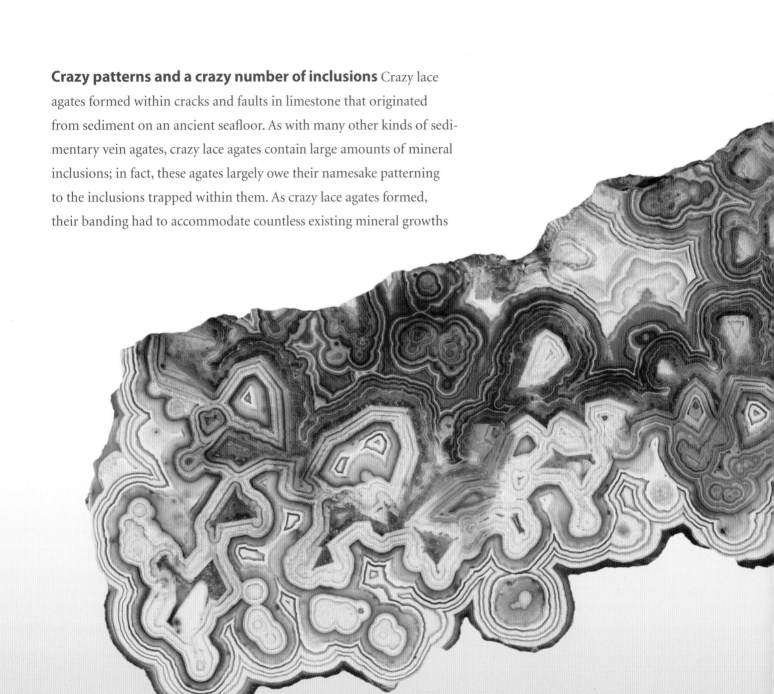

by growing around them, creating crazy lace's characteristic looping, lace-like patterning. This pattern is sometimes so chaotic that parts of the banding appear bubbly, but it can vary a great deal. Some specimens have smoother banding as a consequence of fewer inclusions, while others have distinctly triangular banded sections caused by large crystals of calcite that dissolved long ago. But all crazy lace agates tend to share similar coloration. Shades of gray, brown and white are common, but orange, reds and pinks are the most sought after. Regardless of color, Mexico's crazy lace agates have solidified their place in North America's agate history.

Crazy lace agate
The wild nature of this specimen's banding makes it a quintessential example

Crazy lace agate eyes Though named for their wild, densely packed patterns, Chihuahua, Mexico's, crazy lace agates are also hosts to agate eyes, though in most specimens you may have to look carefully. In these agates, eyes are uncommon, and since crazy lace agates formed as veins within rock, their eyes don't seem to have developed in quite the same way as in agates that formed within vesicles, or gas bubbles.

Most examples lack the isolated, hemispheric quality of normal agate eyes and instead appear to be botryoidal (or grape-like) "lumps" along a regular agate layer. In other words, instead of being a half-sphere "floating" in chalcedony, an eye is a bulge in an otherwise normal layer of chalcedony. (To get an idea of what this looks like, think of pushing a finger into the side of a balloon, creating a lump in its inner surface.) By strict definition, this means they aren't true agate eyes, but even so they have always been identified as such. In any case, they are a unique and peculiar feature of crazy lace agates.

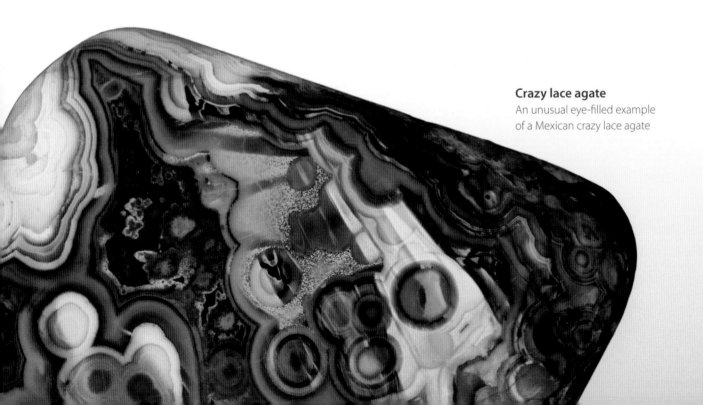

Crazy lace agate
An unusual eye-filled example of a Mexican crazy lace agate

Crazy lace agate
It's not always apparent that these
agates formed as veins in rock

A simple explanation for complexity Crazy lace
agates have long been among the most famous, valuable
and important varieties of agates in all of North America,
so it's interesting that most collectors don't realize the
source of their copious wild, lace-like bands. As men-
tioned previously, crazy lace agates owe their namesake
patterning to the presence of mineral inclusions within
them. Perhaps it is difficult for some collectors to believe
that a few irregular growths of clay, calcite and other soft,
seemingly innocuous minerals could produce such
amazing patterns as those seen in crazy lace agates. But
it's true, and as the layers of chalcedony developed, these
inclusions caused the banding to bend and warp in
beautiful and interesting ways, developing the complex
banding for which crazy lace is renowned.

Laguna agate
Often sold in cut pairs, Mexico's laguna agates can be intensely colorful

Laguna agates

Without question, Mexico's laguna agates are one of North America's best-known and most valuable agate varieties. Mexico's laguna agates are prized around the world, and museum-grade specimens frequently fetch thousands of dollars. Generally just called lagunas, they are mined in the Mexican state of Chihuahua on private ranches where they are found in weathered andesite, a type of rock that forms primarily in coastal volcanic regions.

Limited access for collectors But in the areas where lagunas are found, landowners are notoriously reluctant to allow collectors on their property, sometimes requiring years or even decades of convincing before they will grant permission, if they ever do at all. This severely limited access exaggerates the rarity of lagunas and boosts their desirability tenfold. But that's not to say that their fame isn't well deserved; laguna fortification agates are considered among the most beautiful agates in North America.

Specimens often free from damage These most famous and stunning of Mexican agates are considerably younger than many other varieties of North American agates and have therefore undergone far less weathering. As a result, many specimens still appear as though they were just formed and are free of damage and fracturing, which is part of the reason why they can command such exorbitant prices. Of course, their condition wouldn't matter much if they weren't attractive to begin with, but many lagunas exemplify fortification patterning, often with vivid coloration accenting their bold banding. They also offer tremendous variation from specimen to specimen; if you selected two specimens at random, one might be red with tight banding and a hollow center while the other may be yellow and have large embedded mineral inclusions. Among serious collectors, there is even a "correct" way of preparing a laguna agate: its face is cut perfectly flat and polished to a glassy shine while the backside is left rough and in its natural state.

Laguna agate
Though half the specimen is not banded, the gorgeous pattern makes up for it

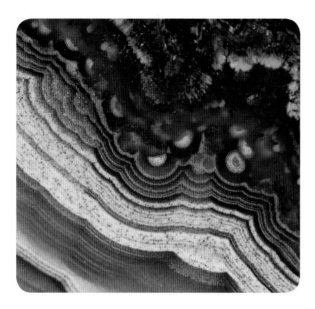

Laguna agate
Though not known for them, many laguna agates contain tiny eyes on their edges

Overlooked agate eyes Laguna agates' bright colors, perfect patterns and generally undamaged appearance tend to take precedence over all other features. But if you look closely, many specimens do in fact contain agate eyes, some of which are quite perfectly developed, albeit small. Unlike eye agates from other localities, laguna agates tend to be so unweathered that the eyes are not visible until a specimen is cut open. This results in the eyes being seen in cross-section, offering an interesting glimpse into how the little hemispheres affect the nearby banding. Like bubbles on the side of a glass of water, eyes in laguna agates aren't paid much attention, but they offer an interesting diversion for those who take the time to look closer.

Laguna agate
More-vivid central coloration is likely caused by impurity-rich conditions later in the agate's growth

Laguna agate
This interesting and drastic change in coloration
suggests a dramatic change of some kind during
the agate's formation

Laguna agate
Stunning and vivid colors are one of
the main draws of laguna agates

The most colorful of them all Although nearly all of Mexico's
agates are vibrant and colorful, lagunas take the cake. Specimens can
be found in quite literally any color of the rainbow, with some that
are unusually vibrant due to a very high concentration of mineral
impurities and others that are beautifully subdued. Several color
combinations are particularly desirable, such as red and black or
purple and pink. Brightly colored lagunas with fine banding are so
coveted—and likely always will be—that purchasing one, as expensive
as they can be, is not only a beautiful addition to your collection but
a good investment. Then again, when it comes to laguna agates, there is
almost no such thing as unpleasant coloration, and well-patterned
specimens will always retain value.

Laguna moss agates By now, it should be clear that lagunas are not only the agate "celebrities" of Mexico, but they are also one of the premier agate varieties in all of North America. Their gorgeous patterning and flawless condition elevate them to legendary status. But not all are such ideal, perfectly banded specimens. Many contain inclusions such as moss. While they may not be as desirable or as valuable as their well-banded counterparts, laguna moss agates can be just as colorful, sometimes with portions of moss gracefully changing color as they extend throughout the specimen. The most beautiful examples show small pockets of banding tucked between masses of moss, but for a moss agate collector, any specimen from this iconic Mexican locality is worth having. Luckily, diehard laguna collectors typically ignore the mossy specimens, making them more affordable for the rest of us.

Laguna agate
Moss agates are not well known from the laguna agate locality, but they can be beautiful

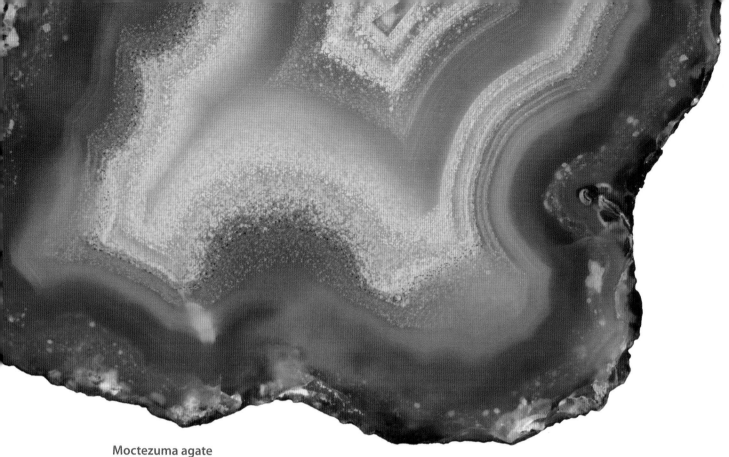

Moctezuma agate
This specimen shows dusty yellow inclusions
of the iron-bearing mineral goethite

Moctezuma agates

Like their laguna agate cousins, Mexico's moctezuma agates have enjoyed great popularity and value
thanks to their vivid, exciting coloration. Like all agates, they owe their color to microscopic inclusions,
but many specimens also exhibit comparatively large flecks of color-causing impurities that are visible
with the naked eye. This gives specimens bands of color that appear "dusty" and make the agates even
more appealing than they already are.

Mexican coconut agates
With its pale interior and dark exterior,
this is a textbook example

Mexican coconut agates

The names of agate varieties can be interesting and even humorous, as anyone
in the hobby no doubt knows, but they're almost always apt. Some agates are
named for the locality where they are found, others for their discoverer, but
many are named for a key feature. Mexican "coconuts" are named for their surprising similarity to coconut palm seeds, and most are nearly perfectly round
with brown or gray rough exteriors and white interiors. Most of Las Choyas,
Chihuahua's, "coconuts" are hollow geodes lined with quartz or amethyst
crystals and other minerals, and many contain little banding. The majority of
collectors who seek these famous and valuable specimens are geode enthusiasts
who prefer hollow specimens, but those of us who collect agates are in luck as
well. A small percentage of specimens are solid agate, most with tightly packed,
hair-thin banding in shades of gray, blue and white.

Red hot thunder eggs

In agate-rich Chihuahua, Mexico, thunder eggs called "red hots" were once mined along the border, near Sonora. Named for their vivid pepper-red and orange colors, red hot thunder eggs aren't widely known, nor are they common in collections. Eagle-eyed collectors will note that red hot thunder eggs often contain some particularly interesting agate eyes; specimens often feature a myriad of small eyes that are clustered together like bubbles in boiling water. These eyes are arranged along the surfaces of chalcedony layers.

Red Hot thunder egg
Very close inspection of these agates often reveals hundreds of tiny bubbly eyes

The Wonder of Agates: Why We Collect Agates

The agate shown here is a fire agate found near Tucson, Arizona, which exhibits the colorful iridescence for which these stones are so famous and valuable. This is caused by microscopically thin coatings of botryoidal (lumpy, grape-like) chalcedony layered together, each rich with inclusions of iron minerals, hence the general brown coloration. When light enters the translucent chalcedony, it bounces between the inclusions within the countless thin layers and refracts, producing the gorgeous iridescence. But fire agates don't look like other agates; they don't show a concentric pattern—rather, they don't have bands at all—and they didn't form as nodules (rounded formations) or veins like other agates, so why are they agates?

As with many other valuable rocks and minerals, agates have enjoyed a long history of collectibility, and along with that history comes tradition. Though agates today are defined as "the concentrically banded variety of chalcedony," some of what we call "agates" fall short of that technical definition. Examples include moss agates, plume agates and fire agates. This is almost entirely due to tradition. For decades, and even still today, some collectors and agate enthusiasts don't distinguish between banded and unbanded chalcedony and label virtually any kind of microcrystalline quartz as an "agate." In many cases, this is acceptable; moss agates, for example, formed largely in the same environments as normal agates, but had a large amount of inclusions during formation that affected the final outcome. Fire agates, on the other hand, would perhaps be better labelled as "layered chalcedony." Then again, that doesn't have quite the same appeal to it. Calling something an "agate" gives it innate value and importance, even if the only similarity between something like a fortification agate and a fire agate is the fact that they both consist of chalcedony.

Agates don't carry with them any major economic importance and are no longer culturally significant in any real capacity; they are merely beautiful quartz formations of somewhat nebulous definition. Yet the word "agate" still carries weight. We want to possess them, to appreciate them and polish, cut and even wear them. We even want to label things "agates" that technically aren't. But we can't explain agates scientifically, at least not yet. Maybe it's our inborn human curiosity, combined with our desire for beautiful objects, but agates excite a sense of wonder within us that only the natural world can. And for that reason, we'll always collect agates, in North America and everywhere else.

Western Texas agate
A colorful, interesting specimen like this exemplifies what agate collectors find so irresistible

Glossary

Agate: The concentrically banded variety of chalcedony

Amygdaloidal agate: Agates formed in vesicles within volcanic rocks and thought to result from hot, mineral-rich water rising from the earth

Andesite: A volcanic rock with a mineral composition intermediate between those of basalt and rhyolite

Band: A distinct visible layer within a mineral formation

Barite: A soft mineral consisting of barium, sulfur and oxygen that forms blade-like crystals

Basalt: A dark gray or black iron-rich rock formed by lava spilled onto the earth's surface

Calcite: Calcium carbonate; a soft, calcium-rich mineral that forms six-sided pointed crystals

Carnelian: Red or reddish orange chalcedony, with or without banding

Chalcedony: The microcrystalline variety of quartz composed of microscopic plate-like crystals arranged into parallel stacks; it resembles fibers when viewed edge-on

Chert: A rock consisting primarily of tightly compacted microscopic quartz grains and clay

Chlorite: A soft, dark green to black mineral that often forms as a lining within vesicles

Coldwater agate: see sedimentary agate

Compound (chemical): A substance composed of two or more elements

Concentric: Circular shapes that share the same center

Concretion: Spherical formations of rock formed around a central point

Crystal: A solid body with a repeating atomic structure formed when an element or compound solidifies

Crystallization: Forming a crystal; a mineral solution solidifying to form a distinctly structured unit

Druse: A mineral crust consisting of many small crystal points, particularly quartz

Element: A substance that cannot be broken down further; elements are the primary constituents of matter

Erosion: Wearing away due to weathering

Geode: A hollow, rounded rock or mineral formation

Glacial till: The rock, gravel and sand deposited by melting glaciers

Glacier: A slow-moving mass of ice formed in cold climates by the compaction of snow

Goethite: A brownish yellow hydrous iron oxide

Granite: A coarse-grained rock formed deep within the earth; most of the earth's crust consists of granite

Hematite: A common, red to black metallic iron oxide

Host rock: see matrix

Husk: Nickname for the thick, outermost chalcedony band of an agate

Impurity: A foreign mineral within a host mineral that often changes the properties of the host, including its color

Inclusion: A crystal or other mineral formation embedded within a larger mass of another mineral

Jasper: The colored varieties of chert

Lapidary: The art of cutting and polishing stones; one who cuts and polishes stones

Lava: Molten rock that has erupted onto the earth's surface

Limestone: A soft, sedimentary rock comprised primarily of calcite

Massive: Occurring in solid, compact concentrations

Matrix: The rock in which a mineral forms

Microcrystalline: A mineral formation composed of a mass of crystals that are too small to see individually

Mineral: A naturally occurring chemical compound or element that solidifies with a definite internal crystal structure

Molecule: A group of atoms bonded together

Nodule: A rounded, compact mineral formation, often said of a whole, unbroken agate

Oxidation: The action of an element or mineral combining with oxygen to produce another substance; also oxidize

Quartz: Hard, white or colorless mineral formed of silicon dioxide; the single most common mineral on earth

Replacement: A mineral that has taken the place and form of an older mineral, particularly as a result of weathering

Rhyolite: A light-colored quartz-rich rock that formed when lava spilled onto the earth's surface

Rock: A massive aggregate of many intergrown mineral grains

Sagenite: A general term for needle-like inclusions in an agate; agates with sagenite are said to be sagenitic

Sedimentary agate: Agates formed within sedimentary rocks as a result of mineral-rich water percolating through it

Silica: Silicon dioxide molecules, often in the form of quartz, or when dissolved in a solution

Thunder egg agate: Round, rock-coated agates formed within pockets made by expanding gases in volcanic rocks, particularly tuff

Tuff: A volcanic rock composed primarily of compacted volcanic ash

Vesicle: A cavity created in volcanic rock by a gas bubble trapped when the rock solidified

Volcanic: Relating to volcanoes and molten rock from within the earth; said of rocks created by the solidification of molten rock

Volcanic ash: Pulverized rock particles created during violent volcanic eruptions

Waxy: A mineral with the reflectivity of wax

Weathering: Being subjected to the forces of nature, including wind, water, and ice

Zeolite: A large group of soft silica, aluminum, alkali and water-bearing minerals that form as a result of groundwater affecting volcanic rocks, particularly basalt

Bibliography and Recommended Reading

Bates, Robert L., editor. *Dictionary of Geological Terms, 3rd Edition*. New York: Anchor Books, 1984.

Carlson, Michael R. *The Beauty of Banded Agates: An Exploration of Agates from Eight Major Worldwide Sites*. Edina: Fortification Press, 2002.

Chesteman, Charles W. *The Audubon Society Field Guide to North American Rocks and Minerals*. New York: Knopf, 1979.

Clark, Roger. *South Dakota's Fairburn Agate*. Appleton: Silverwind Agates, 1998.

Cross, Brad L. and Zeitner, June Culp. *Geodes: Nature's Treasures*. Baldwin Park: Gem Guides Book Company, 2006.

Lynch, Dan R. and Lynch, Bob. *Agates of Lake Superior*. Cambridge: Adventure Publications, 2011.

Marshall, John D. *The "Other" Lake Superior Agates*. Beaverton: Llao Rock Publications, 2003.

Moxon, T. *Agate: Microstructure and Possible Origin*. Auckley, South Yorkshire, England: Terra Publications, 1996.

Moxon, T. *Studies on Agate: Microscopy, Spectroscopy, Growth, High Temperature and Possible Origin*. Auckley, South Yorkshire, England: Terra Publications, 2009.

Pabian, Roger K. and Zarins, Andrejs. *Banded Agates: Origins and Inclusions*. Lincoln: University of Nebraska, 1994.

Pabian, Roger K., et al. *Agates: Treasures of the Earth*. Buffalo: Firefly Books, 2006.

Zenz, Johann. *Agates*. Haltern, Germany: Rainer Bode, 2005.

Index

About the Authors

Dan R. Lynch grew up in Two Harbors, Minnesota, spending years in Agate City, his parents' rock shop, surrounded by rocks and learning by experience the nuances of collecting and identifying minerals. Always with an eye for detail, his lifelong love of art and nature lent itself to an appreciation of mineral formations and crystal shapes from both a scientific and aesthetic point of view. As a graduate of art and photography from the University of Minnesota Duluth, Dan combined all the aspects of his life in 2007 when he began writing a series of rock and mineral field guides with his father, Bob Lynch, a respected veteran of Lake Superior's agate collecting community. Now, Dan spearheads their book projects and prides himself on helping budding collectors "decode" the complexities of geology and mineral identification while also photographing specimens so that they appear exactly as they do in person. Encouraged by his wife, Julie, he works as a writer and photographer.

Bob Lynch is a lapidary and silversmith living and working in Two Harbors, Minnesota. A jeweler most of his life, Bob started cutting and polishing rocks and minerals in the early 1970s for use in his work. From there, a lifelong interest began, and when he moved from Douglas, Arizona, to Two Harbors in 1982, his eyes were opened to the Lake Superior area's entirely different world of minerals—especially the agates. In 1992, Bob and wife Nancy acquired Agate City Rock Shop, a family business founded in 1962 by Nancy's grandfather, Art Rafn. They revitalized the store, and since then Bob has made a name for himself as a highly acclaimed agate polisher and as an expert resource for agate collectors seeking advice. Now, Bob and Nancy keep Agate City Rocks and Gifts open year-round and are the leading source for Lake Superior agates, with more on display and for sale than any other shop in the country.